For Bill Mason —
My very best wishes
to my favorite 'bone
doctor,' and thanks for
sharing this splendid
ritual with me —

WM Brunse

11/21/03

A
Knack for
Knowing
Things

DON BOXMEYER

A Knack for Knowing Things

Stories from St. Paul Neighborhoods and Beyond

MINNESOTA HISTORICAL SOCIETY PRESS

© 2003 by the Minnesota Historical Society. All rights reserved. No part of this book may be used or reproduced in any manner whatsoever without written permission except in the case of brief quotations embodied in critical articles and reviews. For information, write to the Minnesota Historical Society Press, 345 Kellogg Blvd. W., St. Paul, MN 55102-1906.

www.mnhs.org/mhspress

The Minnesota Historical Society Press is a member of the Association of American University Presses.

Manufactured in the United States of America

10 9 8 7 6 5 4 3 2 1

♾ The paper used in this publication meets the minimum requirements of the American National Standard for Information Sciences—Permanence for Printed Library Materials, ANSI Z39.48-1984.

International Standard Book Number
0-87351-465-3

Library of Congress Cataloging-in-Publication Data

Boxmeyer, Don (Donald Harold), 1941–
    A knack for knowing things : stories from St. Paul neighborhoods and beyond / Don Boxmeyer.
        p.   cm.
    ISBN 0-87351-465-3 (alk. paper)
    1. Saint Paul (Minn.)—Social life and customs—Anecdotes.
    2. Saint Paul (Minn.)—Ethnic relations—Anecdotes.
    3. Saint Paul (Minn.)—Biography —Anecdotes.
    4. Ethnic neighborhoods— Minnesota—Saint Paul— Anecdotes.
    5. Minorities—Minnesota— Saint Paul—Anecdotes.
    I. St. Paul pioneer press (Saint Paul, Minn. : 1909)
    II. Title.
F614.S4B69 2003
977.6′581053′0922—dc21
                    2003005087

For Kathy, the keeper of the light in my life

A Knack for Knowing Things

A Knack for Knowing Things

A Small Town on the Prairie

Preface

"I KNOW YOU WANT TO BE A COLUMNIST,"
my editor at the *St. Paul Pioneer Press,* Bill Cento, said many
years ago. "Everyone wants to be a columnist. So, what are
you going to write about?"

I hadn't the foggiest. But after more than fifteen years of
covering hard news, there had to be something about which
I could pontificate. The only subject that immediately came
to mind was taxicabs. "Swell," Cento said. "You'll write about
taxis. What'll you do next week?"

And I don't remember what I wrote about in my second
column, or my third, or fourth. I suppose I gave the governor
hell for something, or the mayor, or the city council. That was
always easy enough to do, especially in Minnesota, where odd-
ball politics are a year-round sport, and those who hold public
office make nice, round, plump, slow-moving targets.

Gradually, though, I began to collect characters—unforgettable characters such as Butch Rylander and Stosh Moran of
Ashby, Minnesota, and Bobo Betts, who dealt funny, and Irv
Serlin, the beloved chef of Payne Avenue. I met and wrote
about Crazy Louie, who had a buffalo head and hand grenades
in his store on University Avenue, and Iowa Blackie, the hobo,
who would come around with his latest book of poetry. These
were the characters of my expanding world, those endearing,
enduring, and absolutely necessary lug nuts who keep the
wheels from flying off the buggy.

I also learned that the governor, the mayor, and the city
council could run things without my advice while I was off

writing about Swede Hollow, the West Side Flats, Rondo Avenue, the Upper Levee, and other lost neighborhoods of St. Paul. Writing columns about West Seventh Street steak man Nick Mancini; Stillwater Bridge tender Walt DeYoung; Max Metzger, the music man; Viking Bob, the pawnbroker; Sister Mary Regina McCabe, the pint-size bread maker of Visitation Convent; and the old black railroaders at Wheels was much more fun than being nasty to poor, defenseless politicians, anyhow. And I got to say good-bye to my friends, among them Joe LaNasa, Matt Morelli, Todo Crea, Ted Anderson, and Wes Barrette. That is what is good about being a columnist. You get to say goodbye publicly to the friends who pass.

These people and all these rich places were too good to let go, to lose track of, to forget about. I wanted to keep them close so that I could retell the stories, and as I was nearing my retirement from the newspaper business in 2002, the Minnesota Historical Society Press presented me with an opportunity to preserve a bit of history by assembling some of my columns in a book. The ones you'll read here were chosen from among hundreds of columns written primarily in the last two decades. Where necessary I've made slight editorial changes in an effort to keep the information current. I am grateful to the *St. Paul Pioneer Press* for allowing these columns to be reprinted.

I'd also like to acknowledge a few special people for their help in putting this book together: first, my longtime editor at the *Pioneer Press*, Don Effenberger, who, through the years, has been a constant source of encouragement; my editor at the Minnesota Historical Society Press, Sally P. Rubinstein; my son Chris, who lent his technical expertise to the project; my wife, Kathy, for her encouragement; and our other children, Diana and Erik, who are now old enough to know what I did all those years when I should have been working.

A
Knack for
Knowing
Things

Palatable
Pleasures
and
Community
Gatherings

This Guy Thinks Lutefisk Is Finger-Lickin' Good

MAY 21, 1989

Jerry Osteraas is about thirty-six, is married, has a family, works in a foundry, and lives in Madison, Minnesota. He is tall, lean, bearded, and in every way, except one, a perfectly normal human specimen. Then you get to the fine print. Jerry Osteraas once sat down and ate six pounds, five ounces of lutefisk in one hour.

So, as a reward for his shabby gastronomical sin, Jerry Osteraas is in Poulsbo, Washington, at this very moment, trying to out eat the Poulsbo champion, an unidentified lout who once devoured eight pounds, eleven ounces of lutefisk in one hour. The two will have, by now, squared off in some insane Viking ritual to determine who can withstand the most misery and discomfort.

I certainly don't want to make it appear as though I'm criticizing lutefisk, but I am. I believe it is only proper for someone like myself, who feels his inherited northern European twinges from time to time, to warn of the perils of lutefisk.

I've done my part. I once tried to get lutefisk outlawed. Failing that, it should at least become a controlled substance to be kept out of the hands of the young and the very old.

It's not that I hate lutefisk, it's just that I can't stand the thought of it. An old friend, Al Nye, runs a fantastically successful Polish restaurant on the edge of North Minneapolis. He started it as a saloon about forty years ago. He saw some promise in the young business, but he had a problem: Among his noontime clientele were several laborers from a nearby lutefisk plant.

Al didn't want to run the lutefisk makers out of his joint, but the smell they brought in with them was chasing all of his other customers away, even after he got the fish workers to congregate at the far end of the bar.

Al was contemplating the failure of his business when one of those rare acts of good fortune occurred. The lutefisk plant burned down. Al thought he had died and gone to heaven.

But then he learned one of the dirty little secrets of lutefisk. Two years after the plant was gone, the smell of lutefisk still lingered heavily in his saloon. If you go in there today and stand at the southwest corner of the long bar in the original saloon, you may be able to detect the aroma of the cod, all soaked and rotted on purpose with lye.

So this is the heritage that Jerry Osteraas leaves to his children—the fact that he is able to consume more poisoned food than almost any other mortal. I couldn't locate Jerry for comment—he was probably getting his stomach pumped—but I talked to the man who put him up to his foul deed.

Scotty Kuehl of Madison owns an antique store and is a guiding member of Madison's business community. Kuehl said the town is proud to foot the bill for Osteraas's trip. Madison, in case you don't know, is a town of two thousand just west of the Laq qui Parle goose refuge, where hundreds of hunters go each fall to shoot at thousands of Canada geese. Towns all around Madison are billed as the goose capitals of the world.

So what was left to Madison? It had to be the capital of something, and since there are a few Norwegians out there stuffing themselves with badly spoiled cod, why not make it the Lutefisk Capital of the United States?

Madison claims that Jackson's store there sells more lutefisk per capita than any other store in the country. Madison even has a twenty-four-foot statue of a cod, known as Lou T. Fisk, which the community has paraded all around North America like a Lions Club bowling trophy.

Now, the Madison boosters have poor Jerry Osteraas. He will come back from Poulsbo, Washington, next week, and he will either have consumed more lutefisk than the northwestern champ, or he will not have. He will either wave his hands around in the air like Rocky, or he'll hang his head and say, "Vell, maybe next yar, ja?"

But will he ever admit the horrid truth: God, that's terrible stuff.

Italian Renaissance for Little Italy

JUNE 26, 2001

A little slice of land on the downtown side of the Mississippi River was once one of St. Paul's most unusual and compact neighborhoods, a tiny ethnic refuge that didn't quite last one hundred years. This was the Upper Levee, St. Paul's "Little Italy," described in 1904 as "a village of southern Italy transported as if by magic from the wild mountains of Abruzzo and Molise and placed on the banks of the Father of Waters."

It was that Father of Waters that would finally do in the little village of about one hundred homes, two grocery stores, a small school, and one saloon on the riverbank between the High Bridge and Chestnut Street. The rampaging Mississippi this year brought back memories of those floods that the Upper Levee residents seemed to accept and endure with a certain measure of poise and long-suffering control.

But by the middle of the twentieth century, the Italians who had populated the Upper Levee since the 1880s finally had had enough of floods and all the misery that went with them. In 1965 the last of the levee dwellers had moved to higher ground, and their tiny community became, first, a scrapyard and, more recently, a deserted field of contaminated soil.

Ironically, the Upper Levee was the archetypal urban village long before its time. Now it is simply one of St. Paul's "Lost Neighborhoods," a community that remains only in the hearts and memories of the people who lived there—people like Ernest Ramacier, age eighty, and his wife, Ethel.

Ernie, the youngest of twelve children, lived the first twenty-four years of his life next to the river that dominated existence in the little village. He's also the perfect historian, filling two lined notebooks with the memories of his youth.

"People, places, and things come into focus very easily and clearly," he wrote, "as I filter them through my mind, slowly, savoring every recollection."

He recalled how the men of the Upper Levee went off to work each morning, some as railroaders, some as packing-house workers at the nearby J. T. McMillan Company, some at Northern States Power Company, and many of them as ditch diggers for the city of St. Paul.

"My father, Dominic, was among them," Ernie wrote, "and every morning they would gather to walk to work with their picks and shovels on their shoulders.

"Their gait was spirited, and the conversation was in Italian," Ernie reminisced. "Little or no English was spoken. On their return at the end of their workday, their pace was slow, in sort of a rhythmic sway, and no longer a group, but spaced out for a block or so, and with their bundles again on their drooping shoulders. There was no conversation this time."

The wood-frame houses the men returned to were nestled side by side along the three streets of the levee, like seats in a theater all focused on the stage—in this case, the river. The main streets were Upper Levee, Mill, and Loreto Streets, running parallel to the river and intersected by several unnamed streets that sliced the neighborhood into about twelve or thirteen oddly shaped blocks. A fourth street, Spring Street, was more of a trail than an urban street, and beyond it, and separated from it by a high chain-link fence, was NSP property.

Before the 1880s, the original German, Irish, and Polish squatters lived in crude shacks that were gradually replaced with more substantial housing by the Italian immigrants, most of whom came from the villages of Ripabottoni and Casacalenda in the southern province of Campobasso.

Most of the young men from Campobasso chose St. Paul because of the need for labor to build railroads. The levee grew by "chain migration," described by one priest as a process in which the father comes, then calls the son, then the rest of the family, and then part of or perhaps the entire village follows.

Coincidentally, the other Italian enclave in St. Paul— Swede Hollow on the Railroad Island end of the East Side— was originally populated by Italians from the regions of Abruzzi, Puglia, Campania, and especially Calabria. Swede Hollow Italians also went to work on the railroads or as city laborers.

The Upper Levee Italians did not always get along well with the Swede Hollow Italians, and that may have been because both places were isolated villages.

"Anyone who didn't live on the levee was a foreigner, even if he was another Italian," said Ernie. "A fellow had to be with someone everyone knew when he came down to the levee or he was in trouble. We didn't have a feud with anyone, but that's how it was.

"If he was going out with a girl from the levee, he'd not dare come any closer than Chestnut Street."

Pat Todora is a retired St. Paul teacher, born on the levee about 1930. His family moved around on the levee three times before it finally made it "up above" to the West End. He remembered playing baseball alongside the old Mill Street School and how the balls would occasionally end up in the river.

And once, Pat recalled, the kids were playing ball on NSP's coal pile when the ball wound up going down the stack of a locomotive.

"We tried to get the engineer to puff it out, but he wouldn't," said Pat.

The houses on the levee were simple but neat and tidy,

almost all of them fenced from the neighbors, not as a gesture of hostility, but as a way of saying, "This is mine. All mine."

Most of the houses had two other features: a garden that was just as large as possible and an oven that looked like an Eskimo igloo for making bread.

"Baking bread was a ritual that took place once a week," Ernie Ramacier recalled. "Mother began with ten pounds of flour, some eggs, some yeast, salt, and water."

Marie Josephine Ramacier mixed and kneaded, mixed and kneaded until an entire fifty-pound sack of flour was turned into dough and raised for several hours in a special bread tub. When the dough was ready, she would bake six loaves at a time in the brick oven that Ernie's father built inside a shed in the backyard.

Levee families also had gardens in which they raised tomatoes, the primary Italian vegetable, as well as peppers, carrots, corn, radishes, onions, lettuce, and a few cabbages. After the autumn harvest, the canning would go on, Ernie said.

And what couldn't be grown or baked was available at the grocers of the Upper Levee, Vanelli's, located in the neighborhood, and Cossetta's at Chestnut Street and Ryan Avenue.

Ernie's neighbor, Connie Perozino, fondly remembered the Upper Levee even though she was "a Norwegian Lutheran. I married an Italian."

She visited the home of her then-husband, Dominic Perozino, because she loved to listen to the Italian women swapping gossip and telling ribald tales about their men.

"They talked about a lady who lived on a corner. Her husband would go to work at eight, and her boyfriend always came around at nine. The women would make hand gestures and say, 'Cornuto, cornuto,' which meant 'cuckold, cuckold.'

"They talked about a lady and her man, and how every time they went back in their tomato patch together, she would eventually wind up with another kid.

"But what I really loved to do was visit my mother-in-law and sit on her porch and smell the basil from her garden as it was drying on the porch. The levee was the home of wonderful aromas."

The Upper Levee and Swede Hollow had a couple of things in common. Boys and young men had nicknames, ranging from Hamfat, Eaglebeak, Coalgas, Peewee, Pinky, and Danny the Dingle on Railroad Island to Dempsey, Bard, Muggs, Spresch, Hambone, Muddles, Stinky, Ace, Lefty, Duck, Gigs, Spuds, Hooch, Links, Bench, Rocky, and Nash on the levee. Frank Marzitelli, who went on to be a community leader in St. Paul, was "the Commish," and Bill Maurizio was never known as anything but "Hots."

The two neighborhoods also shared a priest, Father Louis Pioletti, who came from Torino in Italy in 1924. He served parishes at both Holy Redeemer in downtown St. Paul and St. Ambrose on the East Side, leading his far-flung flock with a stern but benevolent hand. He perfected the two-hour Mass in which he would first deliver his homily in English and then in Italian.

Holy Redeemer was the most important fixture to those who lived on the levee, and each Sunday, winter and summer, families would stream to the church up above in a long, informal procession. The river itself provided much of their entertainment, though. On Sunday afternoons, they would line the levee to watch the "mosquito" boat races in which tiny but powerful boats carved up the river.

"When I was four or five," recalled Ernie Ramacier, "my mother would take my hand and walk across the street to watch the tugboats, with their wheelhouse raised up high like a flower on a stem. The tugs going upriver would be laboring against the current and their smokestacks emitting billowing clouds of black smoke. I would say to my mother, 'Vide a flume, vide a flume,' which meant 'Look at the smoke.'"

The levee itself was an undeclared community gathering spot for the neighborhood, where families went on Sundays to sing songs and build great bonfires with the old creosote-soaked railroad ties and driftwood that constantly floated by.

Young boys had the duty to snare the wood from the river, which was used as fuel in the homes during the long winters. They would sometimes run into Brownie, a Cherokee Indian who lived on a houseboat that was tied up to the levee.

Brownie would engage in a wagering target practice duel with Dominic Fabio, the famous river cop. Brownie would toss a bottle into the river and then fire at it with his old flintlock pistol.

"The smoke and Brownie's reaction to the gun's recoil was something to see," Ernie remembered. Then Fabio would fire his service revolver at the still-floating bottle, usually demolishing it with one shot.

Fabio's job was to patrol the river in his homemade airboat, the *Minnesota*. He tried to keep the kids out of the brewery and mushroom caves that lined both sides of the riverbank upriver of the levee and to keep youngsters from swimming in the river.

The river was like a magnet to the children of the levee, drawing them there to swim and jump into the drink from rope swings tied high up in the trees along the bank. The boys would always try to throw a rock completely across the river, and Johnny "Red" De Carlo was the only one who ever made it, except that his missile was a spark plug.

Pat Todora remembered where Charley Jannetto's tavern was and also LaManna's tavern, where the men would go on Sundays to play bocce ball and pitch horseshoes. He recalled the dock across the street from LaManna's that stuck out into the water and how Tony Ferraro jumped off that dock one time to save another youngster from drowning.

Such accidents did not occur frequently, though, because the kids on the levee respected the river and learned to be strong swimmers. The boys on the levee had their rope swings, and they would sometimes liberate a large wooden cable spool from the NSP yard, dumping it in the river and using it as a raft and diving platform as they floated downriver.

Ernie Ramacier was there the day that a young girl who

lived right next door to him went into the water for a swim. He warned her not to go very far out because she had on a heavy woolen swimsuit.

"It's OK," said the girl. "I'm not going out that far." Ernie turned away for a moment, and when he looked again, ten-year-old Perina Mancini was gone. Her father sent divers into the river to look for her, but Perina Mancini was never found. A few months after the death of his sister, the family of Nick Mancini, now St. Paul's most popular and successful restaurant operator, moved up to the West End, never to return to the levee.

For a long time, the Upper Levee did not have electricity, city water, or gas. There was no bus or streetcar service, and the only way kids could get to school was via taxicab or by crawling up the steep rocky bluff that separated the West End from the river.

"We all thought that anybody who lived up above was rich," said Ernie. "They had all the things we didn't: cars, streetcars, telephones, lights, and running water."

And heat. Ernie remembered how his family of fourteen lived in the three-bedroom house. The boys all slept in the attic, taking turns lying next to the warm chimney.

"That's when we appreciated the firewood we picked out of the river the previous summer."

At the height of its population, the levee accommodated nearly five hundred people. They loved everything about living on the river except for the spring floods, and the one in 1952 was the last straw. River water came up through the floors of the houses, damaging many of them beyond repair.

In 1957, the St. Paul City Council decided to purchase all the houses, move the residents out, raise the ground above flood level, and sell it for industrial use. By 1965, there were no houses left standing, and the Upper Levee became home to Kaplan's Scrap Yard.

"They were tired of all that flooding, and they wanted out," said Connie Perozino. "They all wanted to sell and get up above. But when they got there, they found out that living off the levee was not the paradise they thought it would be. My mother-in-law went into a deep depression because all her friends were spread out, and there was no way to get together as they had done for most of their lives."

"The older ones wanted to stay," said Ernie Ramacier. "They just wanted their gardens, their ovens, and their fences.

"They knew after they had left it that their real home was on the levee."

(By 2003, this eighteen-acre strip of vacant land had a more uptown name, the Upper Landing, and was considered one of the city's hottest prospects for development of a residential village that would provide a $160 million mix of six hundred low-cost and high-end housing units organized into thirteen low-rise buildings in what the city was calling an "urban village.")

Wheels Roll at Noon on Wednesdays

OCTOBER 19, 1992

Wheels at noon on Wednesday. The old men come in and stroll slowly through as though it were someone's birthday, shaking this one's hand, slapping that one on the back. Old black men celebrating a life they shared.

Don't look for a sign over the door at Wheels; there is none. Wheels is an aged commercial building in the neighborhood, and on the second Wednesday of each month, all the old porters and waiters know that Virgil Hadley will be serving prime rib, the kind he served as chef on the Great Northern trains. For just a little while, it'll be the way it was.

"That man is Jamaica Johnny, that one is Percy Zachary, there's Chubby Young, and here comes George Todd," said Jim Griffin, retired deputy chief of police, retired from the St. Paul school board, retired dining-car waiter. "Look how he walks. Just like he's still on a train."

There's an easy familiarity and tender respect here, between Jim and George and LeRoy Coleman, a retired captain with the St. Paul Fire Department, now all deep in their seventies. They've known each other since they were eleven years old, since they played baseball and football together at Webster and McKinley schools in the neighborhood. And when it was time, LeRoy Coleman went to the fire department, and Jim and George, like most young black men in St. Paul, went to the railroad.

They were porters on sleeping cars or Pullman cars or waiters on dining cars. You'll still get an argument over which job was better—the waiters, Jim said, had a crack at the passengers for tips three times a day.

"We had the best food, no getting around that," said George, who wound up his forty-two years of railroading aboard the Amtrak, where the food comes out of microwave ovens. George's railroad was the Great Northern, his train the Empire Builder, the top-of-the-line train from here to the West Coast and where the huge cuts of prime rib were carved right from the carcass of the steer. Waiters shelled the peas and shucked the corn, the apple pies were fresh, and the passengers each got nine pieces of silverware laid on linen.

"The Empire Builder was a silver train," said George. "The passenger got silver butter dishes, toast under a silver cover. If he got cakes, it was under silver. First class all the way, and we polished the silverware between meals."

George became the headwaiter of his own dining car, but he never got the top job, that of steward. That went to the white fellow. It always went to the white fellow, even after George's union, a strong union, fought for equality. George could be steward, the railroad finally said, but he'd have to give up all his seniority.

The railroad meant a lot to these old black men at Wheels, though. George still wears his Amtrak cap; LeRoy Coleman has his father's forty-five-year pin in a safety-deposit box. Ultimately, a municipal football stadium was named for Jim Griffin, but he also remembered the days when he made twenty-seven-and-one-half cents an hour, and men like LeRoy Coleman, Sr., could awake from their sleep and tell you just exactly where they were by the way the train was rocking.

Down on the Flats

MARCH 20, 2000

In another age in a corner of St. Paul that no longer exists, the tall and stately priest would walk up and down Fairfield Avenue in the evening, reading to himself from the Breviary, his Catholic prayer book.

Father John Ward walked from his church, Our Lady of Guadalupe, past the old wooden structure that housed Marvin Levine's Jewish grandfather and grandmother. The priest strolled past the duplex of Levine's father, Israel Levine but was called Riley, then past the sturdy Agudus Achim Synagogue and the home of a Mexican family named Reyes. Right around the corner on Eton Street was the home of the Gastons, a black family. Around another corner were Lebanese families, and a few Norwegian, German, and Irish families.

This was the West Side Flats, one of St. Paul's "lost neighborhoods" that now exists only in the memories of those who lived there. Where once there were the families of Reuben Rabinovitz, Jose Ramirez, and Gertrude Bendoski, and Mordecai the grocer, Monsour Meats, and Israel Slovut the clothier on State Street, there is now a modern industrial park.

This neighborhood was called the Flats because it flowed down from the Wabasha bluffs and stretched out as low and flat on the West Side as physically possible and still be out of the waters of the Mississippi River—most of the time. It is the area that extends east of Robert Street to the Downtown Airport. Of St. Paul's eclectic neighborhoods, the Flats was probably the most diverse.

"We practiced diversity before it became fashionable and necessary," said Gilbert de la O, a Mexican-American member of the St. Paul school board whose family joined the migrant stream to Minnesota to work the fields near New Ulm in 1947 when Gilbert was two years old. His father, like many Mexican men, found full-time work in the packinghouses of South St. Paul, and the de la O family settled into a sixplex at State Street and St. Lawrence near the airport.

"The merchants of the neighborhood were mostly Jewish, and my friends were Mexican and Jewish. We were within walking distance of our aunts, our uncles, and our grandparents. Where else would you want to live?"

Lupe Gonzales grew up on Robertson Street behind the Neighborhood House. She remembered walking to Lafayette Elementary School up State Street, by the smelly old tannery, by the State Street municipal dump, across the Black Bridge, and up the hill, out of the Flats, to the school. "All along the way, we'd be joined by our friends. There were Poles, there were blacks, Jews, the Lebanese, the Mexicans, the whites. We were all together, and we didn't know discrimination or prejudice until we got among the kids from the upper West Side. Only when we got up there were we reminded that we were Mexicans."

Similarly, Kathy Larson lived on State Street and never felt that as a Norwegian on the Flats she was something of a minority.

"We looked out for each other. It was a tight-knit bunch down there. I was a shabbos goy (Sabbath gentile), and I helped out my Jewish friends by turning lights on and off for them on the Sabbath.

"We were all poor but we were poor together and we actually loved each other. I feel blessed to have grown up with people from all nations, and today, I'm accepting of all other people."

The center of culture for all ethnic groups on the West Side was Neighborhood House, and many of the Mexican and Irish boys played football on teams coached by Father John Ward of Our Lady of Guadalupe.

One of those who played was Len Levine, Marvin's brother, who went on to become a member of the St. Paul City Council and later Minnesota commissioner of transportation for Governor Rudy Perpich. "I was the only non-Catholic to play for Father Ward," recalled Levine, "and at the end of the week, he would call us together and say, 'I will see you all on Sunday.' He would then turn to me and say, 'Wouldn't hurt you to show up, either, Levine.'"

No matter what nationality or religion, the goals of all the people were the same: to survive, to educate the children, and to make it through the spring floods. "I don't think anyone ever got rich on the West Side," said Phil Ravitzky, who grew up at State Street and Texas Avenue. "They made enough money to send the kids to college. That was a big thing to all those people. That and getting through the floods."

Dick Garcia, who grew up west of Robert Street in what was considered the "Upper Flats," remembered the flood of 1952, "when our basement filled up with water. We stayed in our house for a while, but the water was right up to the first floor. You walked across the floor, and you could hear the water squishing under your feet."

The fact that the West Side is on the south side of the river, and to the north of West St. Paul, is one of those curiosities that makes St. Paul, St. Paul. The residential area of the Flats developed during the late nineteenth century, and activity eventually centered on a settlement house for immigrants, Neighborhood House, which came in 1897, and four or five synagogues, Our Lady of Guadalupe, and the West Side Union Gospel Mission.

The late Bill Hoffman, who grew up on the Flats, wrote

two books about the area. In *West Side Story II,* he described neighborhood homes as mainly simple wood construction, with stoves in the kitchen and space heaters in the living rooms rather than any kind of central heating. There were lots of animals in the neighborhood, especially horses because there were so many peddlers and rag collectors. What the Flats did not have, Hoffman wrote, was grass. "If we wanted grass we would take a streetcar and go out to Lake Phalen for a picnic."

There was no grass anywhere on the Flats, remembered Mike Kluznik, a Ukrainian and Swede who lived on Fairfield during his youth from 1948 to 1952. When the river rose and the flood of 1952 arrived, "We were simply marooned in our house. I can remember watching the canoes go by. It was an adventure, but what a mess when the water went back down."

Kluznik remembered some of the characters on the Flats: Catfish Bob, the homeless guy and his girlfriend, Dirty Gertie. Gilbert de la O recalled Cool Eye and Mr. Pork Chop. Sailor Bill was a one-time fighter, and a man named Herschel became "Squirrel."

Bill Hoffman wrote that every West Sider seemed to have a nickname. The Lieberman boys were Big Bladder and Little Bladder. There was Chee Chee and Choo Choo, Shakey and Pipkeh the Plumber, Whiskey Bottle and Coco, Greenhorn and Goggles. There was Herbie Hyfligher, and Benny the famous flower man was one of the Kitty Katz boys.

Two men who became very successful were earlier known as Cow and Pink Eye. The three Fishman boys were Shark, Pesco, and Yankee. The Hessler boys were Bucko, Yabby, and Ozzie. The well-known civic leader, Frank Rodriguez, was simply Pancho. Cigar Butt Louie was the guy who passed out from his muscatel and burned down Fannie Breslau's Palace, a run-down apartment building where Mike Kluznik lived.

Then there were the merchants. Most of them were Jewish or Lebanese, and there were one or two grocery stores on every block.

"Everyone remembers Kessel's Bakery," said Ravitzky, "and Ben Mintz's Shoe Store. LaVonna Meats had big salamis hanging from the ceiling and schmaltz herring. I used to go there to buy the Jewish paper, the *Forward*, for my father. Two cents."

The neighborhood teemed with merchants: Louie Finn's drugstore, Tankenoff's fish store, Langmann's fish store, Aaron Goldberg's butcher shop, Engelson the shoemaker, Maurice Lerner's secondhand clothes, Simon Londer the barber, Ehrlich the baker, and a "goy," or gentile store, Blair's Grocery. Primeau's Grocery on the corner of Indiana and State Street sold grab bags for a penny, considered treasure chests that might contain a stale gingerbread cookie, Christmas or Easter candy, fire-scorched melted chocolates, brittle gum, and candy wax bottles.

An impressive amount of gambling took place on the West Side: at Blair's Bar, the Silver Dollar Saloon, and, according to Frank Gaston, at the joint that occupied the building on Fairfield before Our Lady of Guadalupe moved in.

"That place was a pool hall long before it became a church," Frank recalled. "It was busier than Mystic Lake."

And after the disastrous floods of the early 1950s, the fate of the Flats was sealed. Hundreds of homes, shops, bars, and billiard halls, the churches and synagogues, Neighborhood House, the Union Gospel Mission, the community playground, and the peddlers' horse barns were demolished by the St. Paul Port Authority. They would make way for a new industrial park and the Lafayette Freeway link. In addition, a new floodwall was erected so the industrial park would not be subject to flooding.

"The Port Authority stole it from the people who lived there," said Phil Ravitzky. "No one wanted to move out; we were made to move out. The day my home was demolished, I just sat in my car and cried. That was my home."

"We didn't know how to organize, how to protest," Dick Garcia recalled. "When the city said 'Move out,' we just moved out. We should have demonstrated, we should have protested."

No one remembered anyone who got fair replacement value for their homes, so the relocation for many families, especially the Mexican families, was very difficult.

"Two things stand out in my mind," de la O remembered. "The money made available for relocation was an insult, but the biggest insult was that after our homes were gone, the Port Authority came in and built a floodwall to protect not people but businesses."

There is, perhaps, one large architectural artifact left of the Flats, pointed out by John Nasseff during a tour of the area in which he grew up. State Street still extends from Fillmore Avenue south to the bluff that leads to the next level of the West Side, where Roosevelt Junior High School and Dunedin Terrace are located. A bridge abutment built into the bluff is all that is left of the State Street Bridge, the famous old Black Bridge.

"My family moved up to Dunedin Terrace, the street right on the bluff," recalled Nasseff, who would go on to become one of the principal partners in West Publishing Company and well known for his philanthropy.

"We had a good view of the St. Paul Airport, and one time we watched a man jump out of a plane over the field. His chute didn't fully open, and he plopped down in the swamps around the field. We ran out to help him, and he was sitting there with his leg broken, asking us for a cigarette."

Driving down some of the streets and alleys of that upper residential area that still exists, Nasseff pointed out various homes and shop locations.

"There's where the whole Applebaum clan grew up," he said. "There's where the barn was for the fire horses. A lot of peddlers lived on this street, and they all had horses. This place was loaded with horses."

In his book, Bill Hoffman wrote about the demise on the West Side of the peddlers and their horse-drawn carriages: "Peddling became more difficult and the automobile traffic increasingly impossible to contend with. It became too much for his horse and too much for him. He was too old and too frightened to learn to drive a truck. With a horse, one could roll a cigarette with two fingers, take a little nap, and even read a paper; but not with a mechanical contraption which had no sense or initiative of its own."

And of the inevitable, cruel disappearance of the West Side Flats, this neighborhood rich in everything but power, Hoffman wrote: "There it stood behind them—the big, empty house wherein forever would be left the best of their lives. Who could understand that it was more than rooms, fixtures, and furniture? Who could hear the sounds of growing children? Who else could see his wife lighting the Sabbath candles and the family gathering around the table?

"Who else could feel the pulse of life flowing through the halls, up and down the stairs and in every corner? Who else? Who else? Who else?"

Harriet Island Beckons Anew

APRIL 6, 1998

Patrick Ramacier recalled those teen-age entrepreneurial voyages as though the 1920s were yesterday. He would shove his homemade, blunt-nosed little fourteen-foot scow filled with Italian picnickers out into the Mississippi River and row them straight across, at a nickel a head, to the island.

And on hot summer nights more than sixty years ago, a pair of tired bakers from the Upper Levee would plunge into the Mississippi from a sandy beach upriver of the power plant and float downstream. Dominic Alphonso and Frank Marzitelli would just begin to cool off as they bobbed up and down, past the island.

If she looks out the right window of her home at the Little

Sisters of the Poor residence, ninety-six-year-old Theresa Johnson can see the place across the river where her Abdon, the love of her life, put his arm around her shoulder and said to her as the soft concert music played, "Theresa, what do you say we get married?" That was seventy-eight years ago, and she replied, "I think I would say yes, Abdon," on the island, on their island.

The twelve-year-old school policeman marched with his schools, Hebrew and Linwood, down Wabasha Street from the Capitol in 1936, down Wabasha through the Loop and across the Wabasha Street Bridge to the other side of the river, where the shipping tag tied to his badge said Reuben Kaplan was entitled to two hot dogs, a bag of chips, a streetcar token, and an endless supply of chocolate milk, so long as he brought the empties back to the school police picnic, which was always held on the island.

And in the early 1930s, an energetic young hustler named Bowell sold popcorn and Hires Root Beer out of a truck that looked like a castle. His father would park the truck and turn that young boy loose to sell, that boy who became Capt. William D. Bowell, Sr., the colorful riverboat skipper who now runs the Padelford Packet Boat Company from the shore of this island, Harriet Island.

Almost one hundred years ago, this place was separated from the mainland by a two-hundred-foot-wide channel and named for educator Harriet Bishop. It became a gift to the city of St. Paul and was described as a "long, narrow, mid-river strip of land that constitutes . . . a beautiful island park.

"Harriet Island is a park unique with every beauty of the most secluded country spot in the city's center," boasted the May 27, 1900, edition of the *Pioneer Press*, "permanently entrenched behind a natural moat against all the city's dust and sordidness.

"The gates of this pure and purifying paradise" would be opened to all, the newspaper cooed, "save liquor, sin and cigarettes."

May 27, 1900, was the day the city accepted this forty-acre gift from Dr. Justus Ohage, St. Paul's public health chief whose last will stipulated that the land be "forever held and used for the purposes of public bathing and recreation."

Everyone in town was encouraged to come to the public bathhouses that Ohage built and supplied with modest and discreet bathing costumes for either sex. Editorialists then wrote glowingly of the pure and cool waters of the river and promised that any pollution in the river would hug the far shore. But by 1920 the river had become so contaminated that public bathing was abandoned.

Harriet also ceased to be a real island in the 1950s when the mosquito-infested channel was filled in with dredge spoils, but the place has nevertheless officially remained an "island" and, at various times, home to a zoo, a picnic ground, the site for Winter Carnival ice palaces and treasure hunts, dance halls, rock concerts, spook houses, boat races, and kite-flying contests.

Most recently, a new six-hundred-foot-long pier was built so the public can get close to the river, but Harriet Island has never fully realized its voluptuous potential as "St. Paul's Central Park." It periodically floods over, and the Upper Levee and West Side Flats communities it once directly served are but memories, flood-plain artifacts from another age. The tight little community of two dozen year-round river-boaters on the St. Paul Yacht Club end of the island are the only people in St. Paul still living in the flood plain.

"Boats don't seem to mind how much water they float in," said Dave Engfer, who lives year-round on his eighty-five-foot towboat, *Columbia.*

Harriet Island, though, is central to St. Paul's riverfront development plan, and in May 2000 the city celebrated the centennial of Dr. Ohage's gift by opening a renovated Harriet Island regional park.

Harriet Island up until recently did not present a pretty face to the city across the river. Its shoreline upriver of the pier was stabilized but crudely armored in concrete. The south end behind the pier and the St. Paul Yacht Club marina was an industrial-strength boat storage yard, and on the north the island drifted into shabby lumps of dredge spoils.

Major improvements to the park completed by 2002 included a riverwalk to get pedestrians closer to the water's edge, two improved marina harbors, and a developed boat storage area on the north end of the island. The historic pavilion that has always been the center of an ambitious park upgrade scheme was renovated, and the $1 million Gateway entry to the park from the West Side was completed.

Other park improvements include the Great Lawn gathering area that stretches from the Gateway to the grand stairs at the edge of the river, the $1 million stage on the lawn that was a gift from the Target Corporation (hence its name, the Target Stage), two floating docks for excursion boats, the new University of Minnesota showboat and theater, and two new ticket-sale buildings.

"Harriet Island is now in the condition to be used in the right way," said Tim Agness, architect with the St. Paul Parks and Recreation Department.

Gilbert de la O is a member of the St. Paul school board now and a member of the West Side Hispanic community that grew up using Harriet Island for birthday parties and baptisms. He wanted to ensure that Harriet Island was tied to his neighborhood, rather than barricaded from it by the floodwall that historically isolated the park, and was instrumental in planning for the new Gateway that links the park to the community.

Frank Rodriguez at age seventy-eight is a former union leader and state representative who also grew up in the West Side Mexican community for whom Harriet Island was a neighborhood park with a fascinating little two- or three-monkey lockup.

"All of us down there were from the wrong side of the tracks," he said, "and we were very limited in our entertainment, so thank God for Harriet Island.

"When I was just a little kid, I'd go fishing there instead of going to school. One day someone tossed a rock at a monkey, and the man in charge said he was going to put me in the cage with the monkey. That straightened me out. I went to school after that."

Memories of old Harriet Island are not limited to those who grew up on the levee or the West Side, however.

Betty Gangl, ninety-four, came there from Rice Street. Dorothy Davis, eighty-eight, was from Ashland and Oxford. Elsie Kernel, eighty-nine, came from the East Side, and Maude Turner, ninety-five, lived downtown. They all live at Dayton's Bluff Community Care Center now, and they all recalled the magnificent fireworks displays from the island on the Fourth of July.

"My husband took me to the dances down there," Elsie remembered, "I think because it was so cheap. But fun."

Betty recalled the little white-and-green porcelain kitty pin cushion she got from a penny fish pond when she was a little girl, a keepsake that she has saved for almost ninety years. "I saw it there in the fish pond, and I had to have it. It took me seventy-five tries, and seventy-five cents, but I finally caught it."

Patrick Ramacier, eighty-three, worked most of his life in the cabinetmaking business on the West End. It's a business he learned at age twelve on the Upper Levee.

There was money to be made on the Mississippi, he learned, because all the families belonged to Holy Redeemer Catholic Church, and they all had to get across the river to Harriet Island for the church picnics. Crossing five hundred feet of river to Harriet Island was a lot quicker than hiking all the way to the Wabasha Street Bridge.

"I'd pack 'em in," Pat recalled, "eight if they were little and only six if they were big. I kept going back and forth from day-break to midnight on picnic days."

When he got a little older—at fourteen—Pat built his first motorboat out of a Model A engine. Speedy, but it would hardly keep up with the racers of the Mid-Continent Motor Boat Races of 1916 when a young boat builder from Michigan by the name of Chris Smith whizzed by Harriet Island in his *Miss Minneapolis* at a blinding sixty-two m.p.h. Chris Smith went on to greater fame as the manufacturer of the world-famous Chris-Craft boats.

Frank Marzitelli, the baker who floated down the river on a hot summer's night, also went on to greater fame as a city council member, state highway commissioner, St. Paul's first city administrator, and executive director of the St. Paul Port Authority, the agency that took the Upper Levee neighborhood of his youth out of the flood plain and replaced it with a scrapyard in 1965.

And that scrapyard, which operated until 1986, was owned in part and run by Reuben Kaplan, the twelve-year-old boy who marched in the school police parade in the 1930s and who still has the tickets that entitled him to two free hot dogs on Harriet Island and as much chocolate milk as he could handle.

Remembering Rondo

JULY 14, 1999

She would be drawn back from time to time to her childhood in St. Paul. By the 1960s, Evelyn Fairbanks was a Minneapolis resident, but when she came to St. Paul, she'd always drive to 532 St. Anthony Avenue for a look at the old duplex that had been home.

"One day the house was gone," Fairbanks recalled. "The concrete steps leading down to the sidewalk were all that was left of my home. So, I got out of the car and sat on those steps where I used to play hospital with all the ants, those steps where I'd sing to the neighborhood, on those steps that were my world.

"I sat down on those steps and I cried. I didn't know how deeply that house had touched my life until it was gone. Have I been back there since?

"No. I don't take flowers to the grave."

Fairbanks is the author of *The Days of Rondo,* the memoir of a girl who grew up in one of St. Paul's lost neighborhoods, lost in the 1960s to the construction of Interstate 94 between St. Paul and Minneapolis. Her book, published by the Minnesota Historical Society Press in 1990, has been reprinted three times, with well over ten thousand copies in print.

Through the 1950s and into the 1960s, Rondo Avenue and St. Anthony Avenue were parallel thoroughfares. They both began at Rice Street and ran westward: Rondo to Dunlap Street and St. Anthony all the way to Cretin Avenue at the Town and Country Club Golf Course.

Roger Anderson, a neighborhood community leader who grew up on Rondo, once described the avenue as "the thoroughfare, the main drag, the main contributory, the focal point, the center, the epic center, the nexus—it was the hub, the foundation, the strip, the element. It was the headstone of the community."

But then I-94 came and took the north side of Rondo and the south side of St. Anthony. What was left was reduced to the status of freeway service roads, and Rondo was renamed Concordia Avenue. Rondo, the way it was, now lives only in the memories and hearts of those who lived there.

"You can always tell what kind of neighborhood a freeway has been cut through," said St. Paul Police Chief William Finney. "When the road is straight, it has gone through a poor neighborhood. When there are lots of curves, it's been built through the better neighborhood and through businesses."

Finney takes his grandchildren to look at the Dale Street exit sign alongside the eastbound lane of I-94 where it took his birthplace on Rondo in 1959. That sign is right where his home used to stand. It is not lost on them that that part of

I-94 is just as straight as an arrow, a gulch that was depressed so that those who are riding by would not see the homes that were left, the remains of a poor neighborhood.

Rondo was named—and the name Americanized—in 1865 for Joseph Rondeau, a French Canadian and an early developer of St. Paul. Its first inhabitants included Germans, Russians, Jews, Irish, and blacks who, by the early 1900s, were abandoning the city's growing downtown commercial core.

"I was born on Rondo, between Dale and Kent," said Jim Griffin, age eighty-two, a former deputy police chief and member of the St. Paul school board. "Back in 1917, there weren't that many blacks on Rondo. From my place on out to Dunlap Street, it was mostly white. Gradually it became more and more black."

By the 1930s, almost half of the Rondo-area residents were black, and though the black population was widely dispersed throughout the city, the greatest concentration could be found in this neighborhood. Rondo became a pantry and a service corridor for the city, and most of the businesses were family-owned and -operated. There were grocery stores here, pharmacies, bakeries, funeral homes, tailor shops, beauty parlors, coal and fuel stations, ice stores, and the cultural hub of the community, the Hallie Q. Brown Center.

There were, on Rondo and on its neighboring streets, names like the Busy Bee Grocery, Booker T's Restaurant, Morris Love's tailor shop, Walker Williams Pool Hall and Grocery, and the Square Deal liquor store. There were Zweig's Grocery Store, Jim Williams Tavern, the White Front Meat Market, Dandridge's Restaurant, Coleman's Little Harlem Restaurant, the Blue Moon, Chet Oden's Liquor Store, Brooks Funeral Home, and the extremely popular Fields Drugstore.

"I remember near us was a live chicken place," Griffin reminisced. "There were live chickens all over in cages, and you could go in and pick the one you wanted, and the guy would kill it and pluck it right there. Upstairs of him was a 'blind pig,' an illegal still. The guy used to throw his used mash right out the window, and you could smell it all over the neighborhood. And that guy got away with it!"

But there were also the churches of the Rondo neighborhood: Pilgrim Baptist, St. James African Methodist Episcopal, the Church of God in Christ, St. Philip's Episcopal, and St. Peter Claver Catholic Church. For families like the Griffins—and for Evelyn Fairbanks as she was growing up—the church was the center of the community.

The center of the community for Martin O. Weddington, now eighty-one, was the Welcome Hall playground at Rondo and Western Avenue where he played football. "When we went to Highland Park to play, we discovered grass. We'd roll around in it just because it felt so good. All we had on our field at Welcome Hall was sand and gravel!"

Rondo was home to the street peddler, one of whom was simply known as "Mustard Green Man," because of the bizarre clothing he would wear as he walked the length of the avenue calling out his wares. A ragman by the name of Singer could be found in the alleys of Carroll, Rondo, St. Anthony, Central, and Fuller Avenues, with his sway-backed horse and wagon, buying rags for a nickel. Singer, according to neighborhood legend, would send a son to medical school and a daughter to law school.

There were other characters on Rondo: an eccentric womanizer named "John da Conqueror," and Sgt. Louis Liverpool, a popular police officer wannabe who patrolled the neighborhood on his horse. "Good Daddy Hall," who operated a famous after-hours club at Rondo and Farrington, was never arrested by the police for anything worth prosecuting. It was alleged that he was so well connected downtown that his phone rang in time for him to vacate the place whenever he was about to be raided by the police.

"There was also the Turtle Club on Rondo," recalled William Finney, whose mother owned a well-known beauty shop on the avenue.

"There were lots of after-hours places because black people

were not welcome in the white saloons," said Finney, the police chief. "Snooky Price's place was open very late, as were other places. I'd have to say they were operated with the knowledge of the police and were allowed to operate as long as no one got hurt. This was for the lower class."

These after-hours places, saloons, and upstairs poker parlors like Noni Goodman's and Sperling's and Jim Williams's place also did something for the white community of the times. It kept the blacks from wanting to go into the white neighborhood bars and taverns.

Paul Wood, eighty-seven, was proud to have been a Diplomat. "This was our club, just for black teens," he recalled. "We'd have athletic teams and parties and dances. We were the leading teen club around, and the saying was 'The Dips always have a ball.' In no sense of the word were we a gang. We were welcome everywhere."

Membership was limited to sixteen to twenty young men under the age of twenty-one. Famed film director and photographer Gordon Parks, who grew up in St. Paul, was a Diplomat, as was Jim Griffin and the late George Berry, the first black to serve on the St. Paul school board.

Wood is also a member of the Sterling Club, the organization that was formed in 1919 so that blacks, who were not welcome at any of the city's fancy hotels and restaurants, would have someplace to socialize. The Sterling Club is still operating.

"That was the country club for the Oatmeal Hill people," Finney said. "Those who lived in Cornmeal Valley weren't members of the Sterling Club."

There were two Rondos before 1965: Deep Rondo, between Rice and Dale, was Cornmeal Valley, and the Rondo west of Dale was Oatmeal Hill. Cornmeal Valley was looked upon as socially inferior to upper Rondo. By occupation, those in the valley tended to be packinghouse workers or unemployed. Those on the hill were mainly railroad waiters and porters and postal workers, the elite of the street.

"There was a definite class system," recalled Wood, who lived on Oatmeal Hill. "It went almost unsaid. Those in the valley did not go beyond Dale."

"There was a definite stigma to living on Rondo below Dale," said Jim Griffin. "This really was the wrong side of the tracks. And it really did become a rough neighborhood by the end because so many people didn't have work, didn't have jobs."

Rondo by the late 1950s and early 1960s was what planners and sociologists would call "in decline," and the freeway came as no real surprise. There were neighborhood meetings and hearings, but there was no realistic way to prevent it from ripping the heart out of the neighborhood other than to lobby for it to be depressed below surrounding grade.

Some of the neighborhood residents still resent what happened to them, but others thought it was time for the street to go so they could at last get some money for their houses and get out, to make a fresh start in other neighborhoods.

"The city came to me in 1951," remembered Griffin. "I was more than happy to sell because there had been a real estate conspiracy that kept all the blacks in that neighborhood. There was no other way that I would have ever gotten twelve thousand dollars for my house and a chance to move to a new neighborhood (in Griffin's case, to the North End).

"In my opinion, eighty-five to ninety percent of the people who got displaced moved to better housing, and some of them never left the community."

Steve Wilson, president of Rondo Avenue Inc., the organization that produces Rondo Days each year, agrees with Griffin that many of the residents were relieved finally to be able to move out of a depressed area. But at the same time, there was resentment that the freeway was being "not built for us but through us."

Barbara Vassar Gray, aunt to Finney and the one who coined the chief's nickname, "Corky" (for his inability as a youth to pronounce his middle name, Kelso), now lives in Detroit. She grew up, one of the "seven Vassar girls," on Rondo and left the avenue, and St. Paul, long ago. She comes back now and then to visit her relatives.

"Every time I drive down I-94," she said, "I think I must be driving over my bedroom."

Iced Whiskey and Boiled Cod

FEBRUARY 6, 1994

It was the coldest Saturday in decades, twenty-five degrees below zero at noon, and 230 Norwegians still showed up for a speech about how the telephone works.

What the Norwegians really couldn't stay away from was their iced whiskey and their boiled cod. Dozens of them were on the phone to Prom Center before the sun was even up that Saturday morning, demanding to know if Norske Torske was going to be canceled and if they'd have to go without their torsk and aquavit just because of a little cool weather.

The city would have to be twenty feet under water for Norske Torske to be canceled. Norske Torske Klubben is one of the most successful social organizations this city has ever seen, possibly because its mission is not terribly complex. If you want to be a member of Norske Torske, you really ought to be a male, a Norwegian, and fond of boiled fish and a whiskey primarily thought of as ship's ballast.

Someone once bravely suggested that a white plate full of peeled, boiled potatoes and skinned, boiled fish lacks culinary interest. It took a special meeting of the Norske Torske board of directors to add a sprig of parsley, and the vote was said to be far from unanimous.

The Givens family of catering renown has kept Norske Torske at the old Prom ballroom and later the Prom Center for almost its entire lifetime because the Prom understands the cookery of torsk.

Norske Torkse's unvarying monthly appetite demands two hundred pounds of cod so freshly taken from the Atlantic Ocean that fog horns blow when the fish is uncrated. A few days before the January meeting, fishing boats weren't even going out to the banks off Newfoundland because of a dreadful storm. No one had any of the fresh cod, even though the Saturday-noon ritual is fueled by one simple rule: If it swims on Thursday, it is devoured on Saturday.

The consequences of a torskless Torske meeting are too dire to imagine. The Prom's torsk chef, Roger Fierst, has been preparing the fish for ten years. The first time he approached the task, he seasoned the fish as any sensible, sensitive cook would. He even added some nice white wine because, quite frankly, he thought it necessary.

"They almost shot me," he said. "Since then, I keep it simple."

Some supernatural force intervened on behalf of Norske Torske last month, and promptly at 12:30 P.M. Saturday, as 230 Norwegians bellowed the ritual "Bring on the torsk!" hundreds of gleaming white plates filled with gleaming white food and the slight sprigs of parsley were rushed from the kitchen. Waiters scurried around the room, filling plastic shot glasses with amber eighty-three-proof Linie Aquavit made from unwashed potatoes, hauled for some ancient but essential reason twice across the equator and kept until serving time in a deep freeze.

The Norwegians don't really demand much more than this: their aquavit, their fish, and their potatoes. Big gravy boats full of melted butter are passed around, the contents introduced to fish and spuds in sinful measure and churned into a dour, ghostly lump. Torske members rise and sing the national anthems of both Norway and the United States, and there is proud talk of a scholarship fund that periodically brings a Scandinavian to these shores and sends an American to Trondheim University among the fiords.

"We are much more than just a knife-and-fork society," said Don Torgersen, an officer in Norske Torske.

But the Saturday-noon meal is the big deal, before which a retired banker is summoned to tell the latest Scandinavian joke (Ole and Sven spot two guys out in the middle of a cornfield, fishing from a boat. Sven says "Say dere Ole, don't you tink ve shutt go out dere and tell dem dere iss no fish dere?" "Ja, ve shutt, Sven," says Ole. "But ve gott no booat.")

This month's after-torsk speaker was a pleasant fellow from US West, who earnestly showed flow charts and wiring diagrams that reveal how the telephone has changed life on earth. The man eventually ran out of fascinating fiber-optics facts and sat down to polite, subdued applause in a roomful of lowered heads. There is, among members of the Klubben, an unwritten Nordic rule: Never, ever, awaken a slumbering Norwegian.

Horace Hansen was one of the originators of the St. Paul organization, patterned after the Torske Klubben of Minneapolis, begun in 1933. Hansen, a St. Paul attorney, and the late Walter Jacobson, a CPA, thought maybe between the two of them they could scrape up about twenty St. Paul men who were Norwegian by birth or marriage and who wouldn't mind a little socializing.

"St. Paul was regarded as an Irish town," Hansen once wrote, "but we soon found out that they simply made more noise."

That was in 1965, and the founders were astounded when virtually everyone invited to the first meeting showed up. Each of those charter members then recruited ten more Norwegians, and Norske Torske (a name settled on after the leaders deliberated over a barrel of aquavit) was born.

Today, the membership stands at 325 men with such names as Petterssen, Peterson, Bakke, Boogren, Erickson, Jensen, Johnson, Larson, and Lund. It certainly helps if you're Norwegian, but apparently it's not essential; there is, among the membership, a Murphy, a McDonald, and even a Tankenoff.

"You could be one of us," Torgersen said, "if you can stand with us and sing 'Ja, Vi Elsker Dette Landet.'"

Legends of Swede Hollow

MAY 12, 1999

There is a deep crease on the face of the East Side of St. Paul, a steep ravine, a gulch, a canyon where the Scandinavians, the Irish, the Italians, and the Mexicans once dwelt. No one's there now, except the ghosts of the lost neighborhood known as Swede Hollow.

The Hollow has not been inhabited since the middle 1950s, but it becomes more important each year in the memories of those who grew up down there, those who cherished the Hollow but whose dream it was one day to move "up on the street."

Swede Hollow is now a fjord-like urban park with bicycle paths lining both sides of a pastoral little creek that runs from the foot of the abandoned Stroh's Brewery on Minnehaha Avenue to the base of an ancient bridge that carries East Seventh Street. The Swede Hollow community, though, extended south almost to Third Street, where it bumped into Connemara Patch, an Irish Catholic settlement.

The legends of Swede Hollow have never been more important or more celebrated than now. Upward of one hundred Italian-Americans gather regularly to relive their youth in the Hollow and up in "the neighborhood" called Railroad Island. The legends live in the diaries and memoirs of Nels Hokanson, Gentille Yarusso, Ralph Yekaldo, and Mike Sanchelli. The name is kept alive in such enterprises as the Swede Hollow Cafe and the Upper Swede Hollow Neighborhood

Association. This revered valley near the heart of the city has also been memorialized at the Great American History Theater in Buffy Sedlachek's play *Swede Hollow: The Lost Immigrant Village of St. Paul.*

The Swede Hollow era began in 1839 when a land speculator and accused murderer named Edward Phelan built a crude cabin at the head of a ravine where the Hamm's Brewery was eventually built.

Swedes who followed Phelan to the steep ravine built their own shanties alongside Phalen Creek. (Phelan inexplicably became Phalen at some forgotten point in the city's history.) They drank of the chilled spring water that came out of the steep bluffs and the stream that flowed to the Mississippi River from Lake Phalen. The ravine was comfortable in the winter and cool in the summer, and in this little valley, according to the Swedish historian Nels M. Hokanson, they found deer, squirrels, rabbit, partridge, duck, geese, and even fish.

They began coming in greater numbers by 1850, and in lieu of land title or taxes, they paid the city a small fee for the right to live in the Hollow, where they could escape from the "bully boys" up on the street who called them "dumb Swedes." This was their place, and they called it Svenska Dalen. Swede Hollow.

New settlers simply moved into the derelict shanties left by former owners, and they added rooms as their families grew. The most important room was the outhouse, and these were all propped up on stilts right over Phalen Creek. Health and building regulations meant nothing in the Hollow in the early days, and the memoirs tell how young children had the task of wading in the creek to push the floating pollution out of sight into a tunnel that led to the Mississippi River. In later years, it was the city's health department that brought an end to the community.

The Swedes lived in the Hollow much as they did in their homeland, enjoying their snuff, potato sausage, pickled herring, flat bread, and coffee. Railroad tracks ran along terraces cut into the steep west bank of the ravine, and the crews named this run the "Skalle Line" because the Swedish women would ask brakemen on the slow-moving trains, "Skalle ha litte kaffe?" (Would you like a little coffee?).

In his history, Hokanson recalls that spring water tumbled from Hamm's Brewery out of a large pipe into a pool where the men fished and the boys swam. Beer was aged in caves cut into the sides of the bluff, and mushrooms were grown in other caves.

During Hokanson's tenure in the Hollow, there were about thirty or forty families living there, most of them Swedish and Irish. Ethnic disputes are rarely mentioned in the Italian memoirs, but Hokanson writes about the "combative Irish boys" who threw stones at the Salvation Army drums during services in the Hollow and harassed the young Swedes.

Eventually, the Swedes moved up and out of the Hollow, spreading out across the vast East Side. It was, by the early 1900s, the Italians' time along Phalen Creek, which, for some reason, kept the name Swede Hollow. Addresses were simple in the Hollow: Michael Yarusso moved into No. 2 North Phalen Creek in 1895; Angelo Orlando moved into No. 33 North Phalen Creek in 1903; Rocco Santerciero lived at No. 67 South Phalen Creek, and so on.

Who kept these records? Those who lived there, neighborhood historians Sanchelli, Yarusso, and Yekaldo. They sensed this was a special place, and many of the Italians who grew up in the Hollow still gather every couple of months at the Country Buffet in Maplewood to exchange photos and stories of life in "the neighborhood," which included the Hollow and all of Railroad Island. The lower end of the East Side is still called Railroad Island because it is surrounded by train tracks.

There were some institutions up on the street that were central to the Italian families: Lincoln Elementary School, St. Ambrose Catholic Church and its estimable patriarch, Father Louis Pioletti, and Christ Child Community Center.

"Our parents wanted to call it Holy Childhood Community

Center, but it came out 'Ho Chop,'" recalled Rose (Crea) Mahnke, who grew up there in the 1930s.

Don Legato, a retired St. Paul police officer, said, "I used to fall in that creek down in the Hollow all the time. I fell into it so often I'm surprised they didn't rename it for me. But I'm more surprised that no one ever drowned in it."

Marijuana used to grow wild on the hills down in the Hollow, Legato added. "But you know what? No one ever smoked it. We didn't dare to."

The Great American History Theater's treatment of Swede Hollow was a largely spiritual excursion compressing the various ethnic occupations of the community, and playwright Sedlachek wove in anecdotes from the published memoirs, such as the chug races down Brunson Hill and some of the pranks involving outhouses.

One of the major anecdotes is the often-told story of how no one in Swede Hollow could go to bed on Sunday nights before Mike Sanchelli's father, Tony, sang "America the Beautiful." Mike's history of the Hollow helps make the Italian occupation the best chronicled of all the Hollow's eras.

He writes, for instance, that no kid in the Hollow ever had to want for baseballs or softballs. When it rained, all the balls lost in sewers up on the street would be washed into the creek. "Softballs, hardballs, rubber balls, you name it, we got it."

Mike also recalled how the mushroom growers kept manure in quart milk bottles, "and it just so happened that Braunig's Bakery on Maria Avenue near Third Street gave day-old rolls and all kinds of sweet goodies in exchange for the empty milk bottles." So the kids of the Hollow grabbed a few bottles at a time and dug the manure out with sharp sticks before trading them for rolls at the bakery.

Paul Pilla remembered another childhood pastime for the Hollow dwellers. After they heard the fire rigs leave old No. 11's house at Bedford and Beaumont, the kids would scramble up the hill, go upstairs in the station, and slide down the pole.

A narrow tunnel under Drewry Lane at Beaumont near the

north end of the Hollow is still the best entry to Swede Hollow. Gendy Yarusso recalled in his history how a peddler brought fruit and vegetables down to the creek several times a week with his horse and wagon and how the young Hollow dwellers waited for him. The tunnel was just wide enough for the horse and wagon, and once he started through it, the peddler couldn't get off to go after the kids who would attack from behind.

"He couldn't walk back there on his wagon because it was full of his wares," Gendy Yarusso wrote. "He swore, he shouted, and hollered. By the time he had gone though the tunnel the boys were scampering up the Hollow's hills, leaving peelings of oranges and bananas behind."

Before his death in 1987, Ralph Yekaldo wrote, "I am not a author or writer. My spelling ain't so good, either. But I try to get close." In his memoirs, Yekaldo recalled that "Swede Hollow was a city within the city. There were lots of Swedes in the Hollow, but then the Italians took over and, boy, it was something. They began to call it 'Little Italy,' and they made the most of it. If there was an empty piece of land, they had a garden planted, and it was like gold to them. I remember when the tomatoes started to get ripe, it was tomato paste time.

"Wherever you went in the Hollow, you would see tomato paste spread out on pallets on a cloth to dry in the sun."

The men of Little Italy walked to work at Hamm's, Vanderbies ice cream plant, the St. Paul Overall Laundry, Seeger's, 3M Company, on railroads, and, in great numbers, for the St. Paul Water Department. On Sundays, the men would gather at Yarusso's restaurant to play bocce ball and moda, a game similar to paper, rock, and scissors in which participants "throw" fingers simultaneously and bet on the total number that will be displayed. The game was said to be illegal in Italy because it produced too many serious fights over the score.

"I still remember the smell of the restaurant," recalled Bob DePalma, now of Red Wing. "It was pipe smoke, cigar smoke, and spaghetti sauce." Incidentally, Yarusso's, on Payne Avenue, is still operated by the members of the Yarusso family, still has dramatic paintings and photos of Swede Hollow, and is one of the busiest Italian restaurants in town.

"Our mothers used to send us to Yarusso's to tell our fathers to go home," Perry Cucchiarella remembered. "Our fathers would say, 'Get the hell out of here.'"

The stories among the old-timers at the Country Buffet flowed like the Paisano wine must have flowed for their fathers. Paul Pilla said, "See that lady over there? That's Josephine Dinzeo. She taught me how to dance at the Christ Child Center. We were fifteen, and she said, 'Hold me tighter!' I said, 'I will not hold you tighter! You're my cousin, for crying out loud!'"

St. Ambrose, the Italian Catholic church that served the people of the Hollow and the neighborhood, sponsored at least six religious festivals every summer at which there would be a big parade led by a religious statue carried by six men. On the statue were ribbons to which money was pinned, and leading the entire procession would be the spiritual leader of the neighborhood, Father Pioletti, who served the Italian community at both St. Ambrose and Holy Redeemer parishes for more than four decades.

"Up and down the streets of the neighborhood we would march," wrote Gendy Yarusso, "never looking to the side or back. If one did, he got a slap on the head by one of the parade officials."

Eventually, and one by one, the Italians and the Swedes and Danes moved out of the Hollow and up on the street. The Iversons moved, and the Ramirez family came in. Mary the Mexican, Mike Sanchelli writes, moved into the Hanson house. House No. 16 was vacant for a while and then came the Silva family.

From the time he was born in Swede Hollow in 1915, Mike Sanchelli would be away from it for just two years in his youth, when his family moved to Montana briefly (they got twenty dollars for their house). Things in Montana did not go well so the Sanchellis returned to the Hollow. When they finally left the Hollow for good in 1937, they received eighty-three dollars for their home.

"We paid rent for the land," Mike said. "It worked out to about twenty dollars a year, and it went to a former sheriff named Wagener who'd bought up all the land."

Mike believed progress destroyed Swede Hollow. Phalen Creek just became overburdened with runoff from the parking lots and paved streets up on the surface. All the water eventually ran down to the creek and flooded many of the homes.

"The people started to move up to the street," Ralph Yekaldo wrote. The Frascones moved up to Collins Street. Rocko Scalze's family moved up to Beaumont Street, and Tony Casle moved to Beaumont.

"One by one they all moved away from the Hollow. The customs they had and cherished were fast fading away. But while they lived in the Hollow, they had some good times."

Throughout the entire Hollow, there may have been more than one hundred homes during the height of its occupation. There was even a saloon, and grocery, and a boxcar that served as a chapel.

Most of the Italian families eventually found their way out of the Hollow, leaving their homes to the Mexicans. There is no written record of their time there, but Alberta (Silva) Rodriquez remembered how close her family was to the Sanchelli family and how the Mexicans traded garlic, peppers, tomatoes, and onions for fresh bread baked in ovens that all the Italian families seemed to have. "Mike's mother and my mother understood each other. I don't know how, but they did.

"We got along with all the Irish, too," recalled Alberta, who moved out of the Hollow when she was eleven.

By the time the community was condemned by the health department and put to the torch by the city in 1956, there were only thirteen homes left in Swede Hollow. Ever since, this unique community has lived only in the memories of those children of the immigrants whose poorness was enriched by life in the Hollow.

Men of Distinction

OCTOBER 3, 2000

More than eighty years ago, some distinguished members of St. Paul's black community wanted to go downtown. They wanted to dine and to socialize, but they could not. White society would not accept them.

These people were literally all dressed up with no place to go, so the men of the community formed their own stylish club in 1919 where they could celebrate New Year's, hold dinner parties, and host other civic and social events. They called this organization the Sterling Club, and for the first few years, they met at the Odd Fellows Hall, which later became known as the Hallie Q. Brown Community Center, on Western Avenue.

The Sterling Club is one of the oldest black civic and social clubs in America, and by 1926, the organization was ready to build its first clubhouse at Dale Street and Rondo (Concordia) Avenue, despite objections from some in the community who complained that it would be "just another joint."

Members were determined that it would not be a "joint," and for more than four decades, the Sterling Club has quietly provided a dignified, comfortable, and secure refuge for its members, many of whom have been leaders of the black community.

St. Paul Police Chief William Finney is a member. Former City Council Member Bill Wilson is a member, as is Jim Griffin, retired deputy police chief and a former member of the St. Paul school board. Famed photographer and film director Gordon Parks is an honorary member, and the late civil rights leader Roy Wilkins was a member, as was retired Ramsey County District Judge Stephen Maxwell.

The club has survived the Depression, war, urban renewal, freeway construction, and other sorts of bad times, and today its clubhouse on a hill at St. Albans Street and Carroll Avenue looks from the outside like a spacious and tasteful rambler with dark blue wood siding and brick wainscoting.

"We don't have any signs outside saying this is the Sterling Club," said President Arne Benifield of Brooklyn Center.

Jim Griffin agreed: "We wanted it to look like home."

Each of the club's fifty-nine members has a key, and on a typical afternoon, several members can be found there playing gin in a first-floor lounge, one of several rooms where card games are played.

The whole building is rich in club history, and a wall of the main meeting room is decorated with photos of the club's presidents since 1919. They range from physicians and morticians to industrial administrators and peace officers. Several men, including Griffin, are second-generation Sterling Club members.

One of the founding members was Clarence W. Wigington, architect for the city of St. Paul who designed, among other landmarks, the Harriet Island pavilion, the Highland Park water tower, schools and recreation buildings throughout the city, and the first permanent Sterling Club quarters at Dale and Rondo.

Early on in its history, many members of the Sterling Club were either railroad waiters or Pullman car porters because those were considered black occupations. During the Depression era of the 1930s, however, most railroaders were out of work, and Sterling Club coffers were nearly depleted. That's when the club's auxiliary, the members' wives, went to work. The auxiliary opened its doors to the public and instituted cabaret-style Friday and Saturday night events, raising enough money to save the club from mortgage foreclosure.

(While there is no specific exclusion based on gender or

race, club members have always been male and black. Auxiliary membership is limited to wives of current members and widows of deceased members.)

Sterling Club members acknowledge that the organization has a reputation as being a gathering place for the accomplished, the famous, and the elite. Its membership now, as it has been in the past, is held at about sixty members.

"We have some members who are about forty years of age," said Arne, "but the average age is fifty-five."

"We've never had a scandal here of any kind," noted Jim. "The fact is we don't want kids in here raising hell."

"The older people," Arne added, "like a place where they can feel comfortable and secure."

There is a cozy bar in the basement of the club, but liquor is not sold here. Some members, however, keep bottles in locked compartments in an office.

The Sterling Club does not take part in local controversies, Jim said. "We've never gotten way out, and we've always worked within the system. We've resisted attempts to change the philosophy of the club to make it more activist."

While some of its members are politicians, the club does not endorse candidates or political positions, except when it sent a letter of appreciation recently to the Minnesota Historical Society when it refused a request from the state of Virginia to relinquish a Civil War Confederate army battle flag.

The club deliberately takes a low profile, Jim and Arne said, except that on occasion it has sent delegates to do a little lobbying at city hall.

"When we go before the city council and say we're from the Sterling Club," noted Griffin, "the council listens."

"You know," the old chief added, "We're kind of proud of this place."

Angels and Charmers

"Bobo" Betts and the Boys

AUGUST 30, 1998

No one remembers the name of the burn victim, but he was all wrapped up in gauze like a mummy. His eyes weren't covered, though, and the poor guy did have one free hand, so Bobo dealt him in.

Bobo the ambulance attendant got this accident victim, this thoroughly injured human being, into a gin game during the long haul from Duluth to the Twin Cities and, according to legend, the patient was eventually running out of steam but not out of luck. By about Hinckley, the patient was dwindling but well into Bobo, and Bobo was not used to losing.

"Slow down," Bobo told the driver. "Slow down and let me get even."

The driver was Bobo's partner and very good friend, and the ambulance ride got slow enough so that by the time they all got to the hospital, the patient was asleep or unconscious. Fortune smiled on Bobo that day, and he did not lose.

"The patient eventually recovered," Dan Betts recalled, "and he even came around to thank Bobo for showing him such a good time."

Dan was Bobo's son, and he ran a nice little family business that Bobo started in Maplewood on Rice Street near McCarrons Lake.

Amusement City is gone now, but not long ago the go-carts sped around the half-mile track there, the camouflaged paint-ballers splattered around in the woods, and the miniature golfers puttered away as an airplane flew low over the park and scattered the ashes of LeRoy "Bobo" Betts.

Bobo died in June at age sixty-eight, and you probably never heard of the man unless you fought a lot or partied a lot or gambled a lot in St. Paul in the 1950s and 1960s. If you were in on any downtown action at places like the Trocadero, the

Wigwam, the Covered Wagon, and Chili George's, you'd get to know Bobo and K. O. Olafson and Marty O'Phelan and guys with names like Ribs Gordon, Tone the Fone, and Charlie the Belgian, who was maitre d' at Alary's strip joint.

They represented a side of St. Paul the Chamber of Commerce might not want you to see. Bobo once beat up on Santa Claus, K. O. got his name because he was knocked out twenty-four times in twenty-three fights, and Marty O'Phelan had two cops following him everywhere, even to the golf course, just to make sure he was not being rude.

Most of the characters are gone now, and Bobo receives his sixty-ninth birthday present August 31, when this legendary St. Paul street brawler gets dropped in tiny pieces from an airplane.

"Bobo was a player, he was in on all the action," said Dan. "And he was very, very good at cards.

"He went into the air force and later said it was the best three years of his life. He became a rich man before he even got to Germany, and when he came home he came home in leg irons but had a money belt full of cash."

Bobo's secret was that he'd not play cards or dice unless he knew he'd win.

Bobo saw to it that he'd win. His old associates hint darkly of rigged cards and weird dice. I asked Bobo once how it was that so many small businesses changed hands at one legendary, ongoing high-stakes game that Bobo helped run near Jackson Street and Maryland.

"We dealt funny," was Bobo's explanation.

As far back as one West Ender named Nick can remember, LeRoy Betts was Bobo, and that goes back to when they were seven and eight years of age, growing up on West Seventh Street, when Nick saw the big kid everyone called Bobo dragging a coaster wagon down the street.

"What are you doing?" Nick asked.

"Collecting bottles," Bobo replied.

"Cut me in," said Nick.

"Sure. You pull the wagon."

And that's how Bobo Betts and Nick Mancini became partners at seven and eight years of age. Nick, St. Paul's most durable, most famous, and most successful restaurateur, still hosted Bobo's yearly birthday party for fifty of Bobo's closest, most colorful buddies.

"He'd always have a heck of a big party, and then he'd come back in my office and want to settle up with me in cash. He'd want to make some kind of deal.

"I'll tell you what, though," said Nick. "I'd never do it. Bobo was too slick."

Slick and tough. Bobo's buddies say that he was always big, very, very big, and almost indestructible, that he'd like to get in the first punch but didn't really have to as long as he could get his hands around someone's throat.

"He didn't win them all," recalled Phyllis, his wife of thirty-four years. "He'd come home with broken legs and a smashed head sometimes."

And while you may not relish this kind of primal enterprise, there was something atavistically virtuous about the way Bobo and guys like Marty O'Phelan conducted chaos. Their battles were all-out bone-crunchers and could sometimes be measured by calendar rather than clock because they'd go on and on and on, until both participants prayed for the cops to come and break it up. But the brawls—after the opening Sunday punch and up to the boot in the gut— were generally fair ones, waged one-on-one and without weaponry, as distinguished from the lopsided, deadly ambushes that occur in streets today.

All of these exquisite characters ran hard in pursuit of their favorite vices, and for some of them, it was booze or women. With Bobo, it was fighting and money. Fighting, money, and food.

"Bobo ate five times a day," one of his old buddies recalled. "He ate so much, I think, because he never got enough as a kid."

The big guy was also a carnie at heart. Bobo ran some kind of game-of-chance stick joint at a carnival in Texas once, Phyllis recalled. Then the cowboys showed up and started tearing the midway apart, stand by stand, systematically terrorizing the carnival folk.

"You don't want this one," Bobo quietly told the head cowpuncher when the gang got to his joint. Then he slowly took off his apron and went over the counter after the biggest, meanest cowboy of the bunch.

"The fight lasted for a half hour," Phyllis remembered. "Bobo was winning, and then I saw the guns start to come out. But by then the other carnies were backing Bobo up and kept it a fair fight."

By the time Phyllis pulled her man out of that fight, he'd taken several cowboys, including a couple of Texas Rangers, thoroughly apart.

"The Rangers told Bobo, 'You've got a day to get out of our state.'"

Bobo was bad, very bad, but not the worst guy in town. That'd have to be Marty O'Phelan, who established all of St. Paul's unbroken indoor and outdoor records for mayhem. Marty drank and fought, every day, every night. That's about all he did, and he did it very well. Did he and Bobo ever brawl?

"We rolled around in the street a few times," Marty said. He's gone now, but at age sixty-six he was a big, smiling, mellow man who'd not had a fight since he stopped drinking thirty-four years earlier, after he saw The Light midway through a 255-day sentence in the old Como Park Workhouse. The sentence was imposed by the late Otis Godfrey, Jr., who had bad guys for breakfast.

"The judge showed up late for court," Marty remembered, "And I scolded him for keeping us waiting. That got him mad, and he started piling it on."

Marty the Terrible was almost a household name in St. Paul in those days—at least a courthouse name. One judge barred him from all saloons downtown. Another judge barred him from anywhere in St. Paul for two years, and Marty appealed, saying he could be legally thrown out of town for only one year at a time.

His second home was that old Crowbar Hotel in Como Park, and in sober reflection of his memorable dissipations, he explained his fame very simply:

"I had trouble with authority."

Marty and Bobo did team up to perform public service on occasion. Ramsey County District Judge John Connolly was one of Marty O'Phelan's oldest friends, largely because Connolly never forgot how Marty showed compassion for a young friend who'd been disabled in a train accident.

"I was running for the state senate in 1958, and those two offered to raise funds for me. They raised as much for themselves as they raised for my campaign, though."

Marty engineered so much pandemonium that one police chief assigned a permanent tail on him to get a head start on any trouble he might cause.

"They even followed us to Keller Golf Course one time," said the judge.

While Marty spent most of his time either in the Como Park Workhouse or in saloon brawls, Bobo was an entrepreneur at heart. He and an associate named Freckles ran a barbecue joint that also sported a full-service casino in the basement. He ran after-hours joints and one of the first naughty bookstores downtown.

Bobo's friend, Ribs Gordon—who got his nickname because he was the skinniest bookie in town and could not be seen if he stood sideways—had a pizza parlor on Wabasha that had twenty-six telephones in the lobby. Ribs the bookie didn't really sell a whole lot of pizza, though, and when cops would accuse of him of wagering, he'd whine, "Me gamble? I don't even play the radio!"

Ribs kept Bobo around for protection. Bobo was Ribs's excellent bouncer because he was so thorough in his work he'd go out in the street and look for it.

And Bobo ran a toy store once. He hired a Santa Claus one Christmas but wound up dismantling Old St. Nick for pawing young women.

"Everyone who didn't know what was going on thought Bobo was terrible for beating up on Santa Claus right out on the street," Dan said. "Santa made the mistake of coming back a month after Christmas, and Bobo got another piece of him."

There is evidence that Bobo cared deeply for some people, though. One of his friends was Donny Evans, who with his partner, Clark Armstead, gave the world Clark's Submarine Sandwiches.

"I ran Donald's Bar at University and Western long before Clark's and served lunch there," Evans recalled. "Bobo would come in all the time and eat, and after a while he called me aside and said, 'You have to watch your till a little closer, Donny. You're a nice guy, and you deserve to know that I've been eating here for a year, and I've never paid once. So today I'm paying, and you can keep the change. You deserve a tip.'

"He wasn't a boozer, though," Evans said. "He was a hustler."

Bobo never drank because he didn't dare. He figured life was dangerous enough sober, and the streets were full of guys who'd love to catch him at a disadvantage.

Ribs and Bobo also drove cabs for a while, with another street character, K. O. Olafson, who got his nickname because when he was only fifteen he learned he could fight soldiers at Fort Snelling and make three dollars a fight. He got his three dollars whether or not he won.

"I had twenty-three fights and got knocked out twenty-four times," K. O. recalled. "I went down twice in one fight, once on my way back to the corner."

K. O. finally got into another line of work—running a card game with Bobo.

"One guy lost all his money one night and came back with a gun. He took a shot, and both Bobo and I dove under the same table, and I got there first. Bobo looked at me and laughed: 'K.O., you finally beat me.'"

Bobo's gambling buddy, the late Andy Tschida, ran a little go-cart track off Jackson Street, and Bobo thought that would be a neat business to get into. So in 1976 he bought ten acres of swampy land on the east side of Rice Street near the St. Paul waterworks and encouraged everyone he knew to dump fill on the property.

Bobo was finally into something that would not get him into a great deal of trouble, and there he built Amusement City, which was a thriving complex of bumper boats, go-cart tracks, batting cages, a miniature golf course, and a paint-splat combat area in a woods.

LeRoy "Bobo" Betts died on a summer Sunday in 1998 at United Hospital after being ill for several months. According to his wishes, his ashes were scattered over his park on his birthday that August.

"This was Bobo's gift to his city," said Dan. In addition to son Dan and Bobo's widow, Phyllis, Bobo was survived by two daughters, Patty Pelto and Diane Thomason, and two grandchildren.

"Bobo was physically strong and mentally tough," said his old buddy, Marty O'Phelan. "Whatever his trade was, he was master of it around St. Paul."

___

Joe Loved the Trip

JULY 16, 1989

"Joe," the timid, little voice on the telephone said, "I let my driver's license expire. Can you help me?"

"Sure, kid. How long you been without?"

"Two years."

Joseph P. LaNasa whistled and chuckled around the big

cigar in his mouth. How could anyone be dumb enough to let his license die for two years?

"Meet me at noon at the parking ramp, kid. We'll go to lunch and then see about the license."

For reasons unknown to anyone but himself, Joe decided this kid could use some help. He couldn't—and wouldn't if he could—get the license restored without a driving test. He couldn't—and wouldn't if he could—take the road test for the dummy. But the clerk of district court in Ramsey County could take the kid out to where the driving tests are administered in Arden Hills. He could point him in the right direction.

"And you can use my car, kid. Don't scratch it."

That was many years ago, and it was the first time I ever drove a Buick Riviera. The first thing I did in the road test was drive down a one-way street and make a left-hand turn from the inside lane. I looked in the mirror, and Joe was almost rolling on the ground, chuckling and snorting all around the big cigar in his mouth. When it was all over with, I had barely passed with a seventy-one, but I got my lost license restored.

More important, I would learn, was the half-day that Joe LaNasa gave to the young guy to whom he didn't owe a thing.

"You got it back, kid," Joe said. "No big deal."

Recently, Joe'd been very ill, and I'd not seen him for several months. But a couple of weeks ago, he had lunch with a few friends, among them Matt Morelli, his very close friend and traveling partner. Matt and Joe, in better days, would lunch in La Crosse or Rochester or even Winnipeg. On occasion, they'd take a passenger or two out on the road with them, and a couple of times they asked me to join them for their annual smelt run to Duluth.

They'd never fish, but they'd have lunch, and on each occasion, Joe carried two quart jars in a paper bag in his trunk. One held his secret sauce of oils and herbs to pep up the smelt they would eat by the dozens on Park Point. And the other jar was full of pickled artichoke hearts. Joe didn't go smelting without them.

Joe would always drive, and Matt would always ride on his right—the Agent at the wheel, and the Boss next to him. These two old pros of St. Paul politics would swap stories of earlier days at city hall and around town. Joe grew up on Grove and Canada Streets in the Badlands, and Matt on Railroad Island. They talked about the old days in the saloon and grocery businesses. They both remembered the butcher who'd wind up his shift drunker than when he started, and it was Matt who finally found the guy's hiding place. He kept his bottle buried in the sauerkraut barrel.

And they both knew old Nick, the guy from the neighborhood who had the red Auburn Roadster. They'd see him driving around, and he never had fewer than three young women with him. Finally, they asked him. Where, Nick, do you get all those women?

"Veddy few eschkape!" was the happy reply, and the memory of that line would make Matt and Joe giggle all the way to Duluth.

Joe, seventy-five, died on the second day of July. It was not unexpected, and I am told that Joe was prepared to leave. At Joe's funeral, one of the largest sprays of flowers was decorated with a chunk of Styrofoam made to look like a section of highway. On it was a big toy car, pointed skyward.

It was from Joe's buddy, Matt.

A Life without Limitations

OCTOBER 20, 1991

"I'm handicapped," said Bruce Casey. "So what?"

The first part of that is a seventy-year-old fact, and the last is not a challenge. It's Bruce's way of getting on with the important things after people are through being surprised, sympathetic, solicitous, insensitive, and just plain gooey. Bruce is "average with limited abilities," meaning he has more than enough of his own marbles but no arms and very short legs. So what?

"Little kids are the most honest," Bruce said. "They just come right up and ask, 'Where are your arms?'—and I say, 'Jesus didn't give me any.'

"One kid came right back with a second question that stopped me, though. He said, 'OK. Where's your hair?'"

Bruce laughed, shrugged and wanted to talk about baseball. No, wait. There was one bit of cruelty that got to him, one display of ignorance that he was not able to dismiss.

"I was in the back of a car once, parked somewhere, and a young fellow poked his head in the window and hollered to a friend, 'Hey! You want to see a freak?'

"That upset me, really bothered me. The worst thing was that his mother was there, and she didn't correct him."

Bruce came ready-made for rude treatment. He was born without arms and one leg much longer than the other. It would have been easy to dismiss such a congenitally deformed bundle, but it was not in Bruce, from the beginning, to be overlooked in a family with full-size parents and average-size brothers and sisters.

"I played ball and hockey out in the street with the other guys. I was their practice goalie, which meant they couldn't raise the puck when they were shooting at me, but everything else went. I'd put heavy magazines up my pants legs for pads, and I even had a team jersey from the Bluff Pirates. We'd play in the street until we got so tired we could barely move, but when someone yelled 'Cop car!' I could move just as fast as any of them."

Bruce has always lived in St. Paul, and his attitude toward life caught the attention of the late Cedric Adams, legendary Minneapolis newspaper columnist and Twin Cities radio personality, back in 1936. Adams wrote, "He's bright as a dollar, right up to snuff in his school work, and guess what his recreation is—baseball!"

Adams described how Bruce managed by catching a ball between his neck and shoulder.

"To throw, he rests on his half leg, kicks off his other shoe, and pitches with his long leg. You'd be surprised at the length of the toss. He's the kind of a kid that'll take the gripe out of anybody."

That was written when Bruce was a student at Lindsay School in St. Paul. From there, he went to Mechanic Arts High School, graduating in the class of 1940.

"I tried to get a job with the old Trudeau Candy Company downtown, but they wouldn't hire me," Bruce recalled. "They weren't afraid I couldn't handle the work but wondered if people would stop buying their candy if they knew one of the employees helped make it with his feet."

Bruce kept looking, and he did get a clerical job at Goodwill Industries of St. Paul. Bruce cut stencils, operated the mimeograph and adding machines, typed out monthly and annual reports, assisted with the payroll, typed all the paychecks, filled out quarterly reports for Social Security, and maintained all the IRS records. In his spare time, Bruce ran the switchboard. With his toes.

"I was pretty young and cocky," Bruce said. "I always enjoyed meeting people and sticking my foot right out there for them to shake with their hand. I found that made me their equal right off the bat."

Bruce's hard work did not go unnoticed. He was named Worker of the Year for Goodwill in St. Paul and also National Goodwill Worker in the late 1950s.

And then he met Nathalie, who, like Bruce, was a little person. ("I stand short and sit tall," the four-foot, two-inch Nathalie told reporters at their wedding.) They've raised three children; their oldest, Tim, is of average height; he's married and has two average-size children. A permanent foster son, David, is a dwarf, as is their daughter, Sue. All are grown and living away from home.

"Tim had it tough growing up," Bruce recalled. "The

shower nozzle in our house is lower than in other homes, and Tim always said he was the cleanest person in the house from the navel down."

Back in the 1960s, the growing Casey family lived in what was then called the Roosevelt Housing Project on the East Side. Bruce had always worked, had never taken any assistance, but even though he was by then an accountant for the St. Paul Society for the Blind, the Caseys couldn't quite manage to get into a single-family home that would be more suited to little people.

Bruce and Nathalie were active in church work and took their family to the American Lutheran Church camp on the Rum River at Onamia. It was around a campfire there one night that several of Bruce and Nathalie's friends created the Casey Home Fund to help the family raise the three thousand dollars it needed to buy a home of its own.

With the help of newspaper columnist Gareth Hiebert, Dave Moore of WCCO-TV, and others, the Casey Home Fund grew large enough for a down payment on a modest one-story frame home on the far East Side. That was in 1967; a year ago last April, Bruce said, he made the last payment on the Casey home. (Bruce and Nathalie have since moved to Oakdale.)

Gordy Hesselroth from Mendota Heights is one of Bruce's friends from those days at the church camp.

"We used to play cribbage, and Bruce would hop right up on the table and take his turn at shuffling and dealing the cards with his toes. A lot of people would gather around because that was some sight to see. One time, Bruce scored a batch of points, and a spectator, trying to be helpful, began moving Bruce's peg.

"Bruce playfully gave the guy the side of his foot and said, 'I'll do my own pegging, thank you.'"

Bruce also umped the softball games and went fishing at the camp. He had his own rod and reel and could cast out a lure and retrieve it with his feet. One time, Bruce and Nathalie showed up at the Hesselroth home at mealtime. The Hesselroths apologized because all they had was chicken and corn on the cob.

"No problem," said Bruce, stripping off both shoes and both socks and grabbing a cob with his toes.

"Those of us who know Bruce well have to remind ourselves that he is handicapped," Gordy said. "There is a tendency to forget that."

Some of Bruce's determination apparently rubbed off on his daughter, Sue. When she was in the sixth grade, her class took a thirty-mile bicycle trip around Bald Eagle and White Bear Lakes.

I went along as a chaperone on that trip, and what I remember the most is that Sue rode the whole route and finished the trek—not on a ten-speed like the rest of us, but on her little direct-drive toy of a bike with wheels about the size of Frisbees.

I asked Bruce if there was anything he missed being able to do. He thought for a long time. He gets just about everywhere he wants to go in his motorized wheelchair, and he and Nathalie would take summer trips around the country.

"The Lord's been good to me," he said. "I can't figure out why, but he has."

Bruce thought some more about my question, and finally said: "Skate. I would have loved to have been able to skate. Without arms, though, I wouldn't have any balance. I used to love to go the state high-school hockey tournament, and I remember one little goalie, Willard Ikola, who could stand straight up under the net."

Bruce, ever the dedicated sports fan, remembered the highlights of his life:

"I saw the first two games of the 1946 World Series between the St. Louis Cardinals and the Boston Red Sox, and I got married to Nathalie. Those are the special events."

Nathalie had a seventieth-birthday party for Bruce at their church, and a few days after the party, those who'd attended received thank-you cards that read, "I sure was surprised when I saw you come through the door. Thank you for your thoughtfulness. I appreciated it very much."

It was signed "Bruce." Bruce had written all of his thank-you notes himself.

A Traveler Drops in at Avalanche

JULY 1, 1992

You'll probably not get to places like Five Points, Bud, Bosstown, or Esofea—unless you have time. I had time—three days to find my way across southern Wisconsin—so if a road sign raised questions, I went there. That's how I found Soldiers Grove, poked around Blue Mound, and bought my wooden mushrooms at Mazomanie.

And over in the corner of the state where the Mississippi gets ready to swallow up the Wisconsin River, I took a quick left off the state highway when I saw the sign that said "Avalanche." How does a town in the Midwest get to be named Avalanche?

The narrow little blacktop road dipped into the woods and wound around the lumpy landscape like yarn on a ball, and I drove down the shaded, ever-steeper trail past old barns and clutches of male cardinals that lined the road like red-coated sentries. The lush green foliage opened occasionally where rock outcroppings burst from the woods like wounds, bleeding out the stones and boulders that lay at roadside. I guessed at my answer before I got to Avalanche.

Then the road flattened out into a snug, sunny valley a loud dog could bark across. Neat houses, a dozen or so, were set back and spread out along the west fork of the Kickapoo River. In a rich, dark field next to the purling Kickapoo, a tractor chugged slowly along, followed by two young girls planting tobacco.

I stopped at the Avalanche store, which used to be the school, and Laurie Widner came out to see who'd come to Avalanche that morning. Why, I asked Laurie, is the town named Avalanche?

She didn't know, but she'd find out. So Laurie Widner went out to the middle of the street and began addressing the town. "June!" she cried, and then "Mary!" The phones in Avalanche don't work as well as the direct approach, and soon June Widner, who's married into the town's biggest family, and a friend, Mary Schunberg, were there.

Why is the town named Avalanche?

Because folks say there once was one, said Mary. It brought down the gristmill over there, right alongside the Kickapoo. The whole hill slid down, according to the story. Mary went to her home and brought back pictures of Avalanche the way it used to be. There was a creamery once, and the cheese factory over there is now a chapel. Then there was a place where people danced.

"It used to be big," said June. "There were five hundred or six hundred people here. There's still about fifty or sixty."

The *La Crosse Tribune* put the population at twenty-nine earlier this year, said Laurie.

"That's a misprint," said June. "There must be thirty-five."

The newspaper story told about the all-class reunion that would take place the day after I was in Avalanche and said of the town, and its name, this:

"Some say it's named for a land formation resembling a landslide. Some say there once was one. Still, it was, and is, the kind of town that farmers retire to, where widows aren't afraid to stay alone at night, and where a dog can snooze on the centerline of the main street. You don't even see bumper stickers asking where in the world it is."

And then I was up and out of the Kickapoo River Valley. Avalanche went on its way, and I on mine.

Matt the Boss: An Exuberant Congregant

JANUARY 6, 1995

It was a very select group that would pile into the Agent's Buick. Whispering Smith in the back, his jaws flapping in the breeze; maybe Farley, the Political Scientist; and Father Leander. In the front there would be Joe LaNasa, the Agent, at the wheel, and in the front passenger seat—always in the front seat—was Matt Morelli, the Boss. He was the leader.

"They would fight and argue about everything from politics to baseball, they'd be killing each other," said Farley. "At 4:00 P.M., Father Leander announced it was time to say the Rosary, and they all asked him to say it aloud so they could go through it with him. For the next fifteen minutes, they'd say the Rosary and then get back to whatever they were yelling about."

This band of merry men would end up in Duluth for a smelt lunch or in Rochester if Joe needed a new pair of shoes. They once wound up in Ontario for breakfast, and each time, Joe was at the wheel and Matt was in the front passenger seat, burning holes in Joe's car with his cigarettes.

This exuberant congregation of some of St. Paul's most colorful characters—some of its most powerful men—is now adjourned. Its last member, Matt Morelli, died at age seventy-eight Tuesday, less than a month after the death of Anthony J. Crea, who was, to his long-suffering, beloved sidekicks, the loquacious Whispering Smith.

When Joe LaNasa died in 1989, one of the largest sprays of flowers was decorated with a chunk of Styrofoam made to look like a section of highway. On it was a big toy car, pointed skyward. That was from Matt, the grocer. The Boss. He was always Big Matt, just as his friend and distant cousin, Matt Morelli the plumber, has always been Little Matt.

The Matt-and-Joe road show was legendary, and truck drivers would tell Matt how much they envied him, running all over the state for lunch. And Matt would tell them, "Listen: If you'd peeled as many potatoes, swept as many floors, and cleaned as many bathrooms and cuspidors as Joe and I did in our younger days, you could afford to be running around, and that's the truth, so help me God!"

The Morelli store on Payne Avenue was just a few years older than Matt, having been started in 1915 by Matt's father, Jim, and his mother, Mary. Matt graduated from Johnson High School and earned an associate of arts degree from the University of Minnesota, time out from the store that his father never really considered valuable.

Matt grew up in Swede Hollow, and until the end of his life he could tell you exactly how many steps led to the belly of the Hollow, because that's where he lugged groceries each day. Later, in the 1950s, Matt and a partner helped introduce pizza to St. Paul through their Matt & Gene's pizza shops. But the mainstays of the Morelli empire were the store and the Savoy restaurant on East Seventh and Lafayette Street.

On the road with Joe, Matt would start to giggle. A Savoy story had come to him, such as the days when he sold beer for a nickel, soup for fifteen cents, and his "tightwad" customers from 3M would eat a dollar's worth of free crackers.

Or the time a customer lost his false teeth down the toilet. Matt refused the man's plea for him to fish around for the teeth in the plumbing but suggested that the customer go over to the Pig's Eye sewage plant to see if they'd found his teeth. The guy came back a few days later with teeth in his mouth.

"He said, 'It took me a while, but I finally found a pair that fit!'"

St. Paul had two patriarchs, said Bob Hess, once a heavy-duty player in the city's political drama.

"St. Paul has Frank Marzitelli on the West End, and it had Matt on the East Side. If people had a problem, they'd go see Matt, walk up the steps to his little office, and he'd help them. He was a leader in every good sense of that word. The acknowledged, beloved leader. That's just the way it worked. If Matt called, it evoked an immediate response."

Matt for many years co-chaired the congressional fundraising efforts for Hess's boss, Representative Joe Karth, and Karth never lost. When Karth decided to retire in 1976, Hess was urged by Matt and another player, Bob Goff, to step forward for the seat.

"Run, Bob," said Matt. "I'll go to the bank and get ten thousand dollars for you."

"Matt, you wouldn't have to go to the bank," said Goff.

With Matt, said his longtime friend, Don Del Fiacco, "It was family, church, the store, politics, and baseball. We never ran out of things to talk about on those long rides."

Six years ago, Matt suffered a stroke from which he never recovered. It left him in a wheelchair and unable to get up the steep stairs to his little office, where his buddies—from federal judges to truck drivers—would come to smoke cigars and talk.

But he went to the store in his wheelchair for a few hours each day, up until just a few weeks ago, said his son, Jim. After Matt was hospitalized the last time, his wife, Edie, called a cab to take her to the hospital. The cab driver recognized the name and told her that many years ago he could not get in to see the right people at Taystee Bread Company, where he wanted a job.

"Dad wrote a letter for him, the baker told my mother, and he worked there twenty-five years until the place closed. He just wanted her to know that and to know he would always remember Matt Morelli."

I was also fortunate to know Matt Morelli for many years, to have taken some of those rides with him and Joe. After the stroke that robbed him of so many things, I mentioned to Matt that I'd never once heard him complain about poor health or bad luck.

"Box, let me tell you," Matt said. "God has been so good to me that if I complained, it would be like spitting right in His eye. That's the truth, so help me God!"

Iowa Blackie, King of the Hobos

AUGUST 27, 1993

Iowa Blackie—I don't know him by any other name—has reached the top of his profession. I remember when he sat on the fringe of greatness while the moguls of the business drew close and held court at the cook fire of the jungle. Now, years later, it's Iowa Blackie's turn. Blackie is finally king of the hobos.

"I will try to lend honor to the office," Blackie said the other day, after arriving in Minneapolis from Britt, Iowa, where hobo kings and queens are crowned at their convention each summer. "I will visit the elderly and go to at least three railroad festivals." Visiting and going are what Blackie does best. Between visiting and going, and writing his poetry, there's not much time left for aimless hoboing.

Becoming king is every hobo boy's dream, and Blackie, now forty-three or forty-four, has been after it since Thursday, June 20, 1963, when he boarded a train in a small town in Iowa and never really ever went home again.

As a full-time hobo in good standing, Blackie was more than entitled to sit around the real hobo fire the year I met him at Britt (the drunks and druggies jungled-up down the tracks somewhere). But Blackie was often off by himself, a spare, bearded, shaggy-haired, bare-chested fellow in bib overalls, just watching and writing things down in a big notebook.

It surprised me at first to hear a cordial greeting and soft words come out of such a malevolent-looking heap, and I learned that Blackie was a sensitive poet hopelessly in love with Minneapolis Jewel, the woman whose name is tattooed on Blackie's arm.

Jewel was queen of the jungle then, escorted, as it were, by Inkman, a heavily tattooed gold prospector from Chicago. So Blackie sat on the fringes, wrote poetry, and took a run at being hobo king against Galoway Slim, Gascan Patty, Alabama

Hobo, and Man Called John; all of them big, big hobos. Blackie lost, but I'd hear from him when he'd blow into town to try the salad bars at new Burger Kings in Cottage Grove or North Minneapolis.

Once, he teamed up with Jewel for some poetry reading at Mayslack's in Minneapolis, and he seemed to be working hard to get over her. He talked about poetry, railroading, and the search for really good boots.

Blackie has a business card, and he's on his third book of poetry. First, there was the blue one, he said. Then, the red one. And now, the orange. He feels really good about being hobo king and figures he finally won because the competition—Knockman and Liberty Justice—was the weakest in years.

Blackie's hero, Steamtrain Maury, the hobo king of hobo kings, is aging but still tells the best stories and does the annual graveyard tribute to fallen hobos better than anyone. "Maury sort of rambles a bit now," said Blackie. "But I'll let him ramble."

Then, it was time for Blackie to move on. But first, he filled me in on Jewel, the love of his life. She's not with the Inkman anymore, said Blackie. She's got someone new, may have even married him.

"She calls the new guy Candyman," said Blackie. "This one's a damn yuppie."

Tony Crea: A Character with Character

DECEMBER 14, 1994

The priest and his golfing partner were teeing off at Goodrich to a long, narrow fairway, and the partner, one Anthony J. Crea, sliced his ball deep into the woods.

"He let go with a line of lingo I'd never heard him use before," said the Rev. Thomas Pingatore of St. Ambrose Catholic Church. "I said, 'Tony, if you keep talking like that, I'm not going to play golf with you.'"

"Tony apologized all over the place and said he'd never, ever say those terrible words again, and when it was my turn to tee off, I sliced it exactly as he had and wound up in the woods."

The priest turned to his friend and said, "Tony, would you please repeat what you just said?"

Tony was fond of homilies that he considered reasonably brief in duration, and Father Pingatore tried to accommodate his restless friend. Even so, Tony routinely made a big production out of pointing at his wristwatch when he'd had enough preaching.

"I had the shortest homilies on the East Side," Father Pingatore said. "Now, I'll have the longest."

Tony Crea died last week at seventy-five years of age, and all over Ramsey County, friends were sharing stories about "Todo" and his huge heart, his bombastic temper, and his ferocious loyalty.

"He'd break your arm if you ever went for your wallet," said retired Ramsey County District Judge Harold Schultz. "He'd yell at you for being a cheapskate, but you absolutely could not buy that man a meal."

"Tony's favorite line when he was refusing a favor was 'I don't want to be obligated!'" said Keller golf pro Tom Purcell. "But there wasn't a person at his funeral who didn't owe Tony something."

In the late 1960s, Tony was deputy public-works commissioner in St. Paul. A young, noisy activist who called himself the "voice of the people" appeared before the city council one day to harangue Tony's boss, the popular Bob Peterson, to whom Tony was devoted.

"I'll voice-of-the-people you, you (bleep-bleep)," Crea roared. "If you leave the courthouse right now, I won't throw you out the window!"

Tony was discussing an issue with a friend. "When I want your opinion," Tony explained, "I'll give it to you!"

His exuberant excesses made him a character. But the virtues of honesty and loyalty gave Tony Crea character. It was not possible for him to take his family, his friends, his city, and his church casually. He volunteered his resources willingly, whatever the cause, and demanded that everyone else give just as willingly.

"We shared him with all of you," his son, Tony Jr., told the mourners at his father's funeral, drawing laughter when he added, "At times, we'd have been glad to give him to you, and I'm sure sometimes you felt the same way."

If one of Tony's pals was in the hospital, Tony would round up all the funeral sprays he could from a mortician friend he called "The Digger" and have them delivered to the room. Tony once posed as a doctor and ordered the nurses to give a hospitalized friend regular enemas.

Tony Crea retired in 1987 as director of parks and recreation for Ramsey County, having accomplished the near impossible in delivering—on time and within budget—eight new indoor ice arenas. His political survival was due in part to his menacing resonance—he ordered Ramsey County commissioners around as though he were the boss, earning another nickname, "Whispering Smith"—but more particularly because he was uncommonly good at what he did and fiercely loyal to those for whom he did it.

In return, he wanted only small concessions for himself. While he was recreation director for the county, the water hole at Goodrich that his ball kept winding up in was turned into a sand trap. The recreation department headquarters that was built under his direction was dubbed "Taj Ma Crea."

He was Todo to me for more than twenty-five years. I asked him innocently one time back in our city hall days where a guy could pick up some of those abandoned two-foot sidewalk tiles. Two hours later, my wife called to say there was a big, orange city truck making a delivery behind our garage.

Having Todo as a friend was one of the joys of life, and his customary greeting would go something like this: "Take your hat off! Get a haircut!"

Then, he'd say my last column was awful, and I'd congratulate him for finding someone who could read it to him. He'd shout and cuss, and I knew everything was OK between us.

I asked him once what "Todo" means.

"Everything," he growled. "It means everything."

<hr>

It Was His Vision, Not His Sight

OCTOBER 1, 1994

We never really knew how much Leo could see. With his thick, telescopic glasses, he could read the newspaper if he scrunched it up tight to his eye. He could make out shapes, we guessed, but the grandkids learned early not to leave their birthday cake sitting around on chairs.

Leo's talent was his ability to observe without being able to see, to navigate by a combination of intuition, memory, and the bus line. When the grandchildren who are now in their late twenties were small, he'd take them all to see the exciting new IDS tower in Minneapolis, shepherding them through the various bus transfers, and like little ducks in a row, he'd lead them, and they'd lead him, right to the top so they could see for him.

Being blind almost from birth didn't stop Leo from working at the old Citizen's Ice plant at Dale and Selby, a monstrous, ammonia-reeking, ice-encrusted cavern full of bubbling vats and dangerous pitfalls even for people with perfect vision. Leo ran the place at night, and when his shift was over, he'd quite often come home in a squad car. He had friends who worried about him.

In more than thirty years of being part of Leo Carle's large, beautiful family, I never heard him complain of being handicapped. His gift was not his sight but his vision. His craft was his ability to see financial numbers the rest of us missed.

Leo put a house deal together for one of his daughters, assembling funds in such a way that everyone, except the bank, came out ahead. He explained it, and, of course, I did not understand, but I knew he was enormously proud because he acknowledged his blindness.

"If I could have seen," he said, "I'd have been a hell of a banker."

He was a dispatcher for Art's Towing Company on Rice Street many years ago and got to know his city from one end to the other, top to bottom. Give Leo an intersection, any intersection, and he'd tell you the number of a house on the corner. We'd toss out the name of a dinky little street or alley Leo couldn't possibly know. Mt. Ida Street, or Preble Street.

"That's easy. Mt. Ida goes from Rivoli across Otsego, and Preble is up there next to Jessie."

Neiderhoffersteinenwald. We threw him a combination that wasn't on anyone's map.

"I know where my half is," Leo said with a grin. "Where's your half?"

Leo and Grandma had eight children who've remained extraordinarily close. No one's ever moved too far from home, so family Christmases and even birthdays have always been small, intimate little immediate family gatherings of sixty or seventy except for those who were off playing or coaching hockey. While it did not have the full support of the patriarch, hockey became the family sport.

"I hope I don't die during hockey season," Leo would mutter. "Nobody'll be around to bury me."

Leo was eighty-three when death came—quickly, unexpectedly, with dignity and, we hope, without pain. Leo had been with Grandma and two of his daughters, and he was happy. He'd been riding around in the country, seeing things.

Serving Up
Goodwill

Surprises in Store at Crazy Louie's

SEPTEMBER 2, 1990

I knew what was missing as soon as I walked in the door. The cluck was gone.

Crazy Louie's Surplus City on University Avenue has been rendered cackle-free ever since Louie decided to fold his bed pads, take down his machine guns, box up his stuffed bobcats, and sell out. The first thing he did was to hide the machine that made sounds like a hen giving birth to a football.

"I sell everything, including my store, if the deal is right," said Norman Tolchiner, who has been Crazy Louie since the store opened in 1979. "Everything but my toys."

Crazy Louie's caught my attention several years ago when I was in the market for a few hand grenades and a buffalo head. Crazy Louie had some of each. There are other surplus dealers in town; the Axman just west of Snelling on University is a perfect example of good product organization where everything has its place and nametag, unlike Louie's, where you were likely to find the forty-nine-cent bed pads next to the coffee mugs. Louie's had several stuffed peacocks frozen in mid-strut on a back-wall shelf, which was so high that the birds' flared tails had to be detached and displayed on another counter.

Part of the mystique of Crazy Louie's was not knowing what was for sale and what was part of his private collection. The cluck machine was part of the collection, as was old Chief Hanging Horn, a human-sized ceramic aborigine with a one-armed bandit planted in his chest.

After Crazy Louie's closes this October, Norm will keep his toy trains, his dollhouses, and his wooden machine guns. Why is the store closing? Norm, fifty-four, shrugged his shoulders. It's time. He got an offer he couldn't refuse. He and his family will continue to run their state fair booth in the grandstand, where they've been pumping out personalized dog tags for twenty-seven years.

Want a buffalo head? Louie's got two of them, one for fifteen hundred dollars and one for eighteen hundred. His black bear is twenty-five hundred, and the black Alaskan timber wolf is not for sale, as is the bus-token counter, the boar's head, and Louie's dentist's chair. My favorite is his stuffed Afghan hound wearing the sun bonnet.

The merchandise at Louie's appears to have been picked over pretty thoroughly, but you still can swing a big deal on "Class of '89" drinking cups or seventy-nine-cent coffee mugs with the slogan: "Illinois Council on Long Term Care." If you're from the firm of Shank, Irwin, Conant, Lipshky, & Casterline, your personalized mugs are in.

One day last week, I asked clerk Gilbert Gonzalez to show me the best-quality merchandise, the no-expenses-spared, top-shelf material that Louie might have been saving for his preferred customers. Gilbert gave me a knowing nod, crooked his finger, and led me to the main counter, where he had a boxful of carved brass wedding rings that were only starting to turn a little green.

"Between these rings and those neck chains over there," he said, "for four dollars, you could be king."

Gilbert saved his best stuff for last. He showed me his top-of-the-line perfume, simply called "BIC," bottled by the same folks who bring you ballpoint pens and disposable lighters. Crazy Louie knows a guy who bought sixty forty-eight-foot trailer loads of the stuff.

"This is high quality, one-dollar-and-ninety-five-cents a jug," Gilbert said. "Guaranteed to make you smell like the old lady on the bus."

A West Side Horatio Alger

FEBRUARY 27, 1999

John Nasseff stood on the balcony of his penthouse and looked out at his life. He could live anywhere he wanted, could have as many houses as he would like. He has just this one, though, on the twenty-fourth floor of Park Towers in downtown St. Paul, less than a half-mile from where he's spent his entire life.

"I haven't gone far in the world," Nasseff joked, "but I sure went up."

The story of John Nasseff is a Horatio Alger saga of monumental luck and pluck. This scrappy, street-savvy son of poor immigrant parents overcame the poverty of his youth by determination, daring, and hard work. If there was a carload of fruit to be unloaded at the City Market, Johnny Nasseff would do it. If there was a telegram to be delivered from Western Union, Nasseff was there on his bike. If there was a newspaper to be peddled or a leather glove to be made, Nasseff could handle it.

Years later, after he returned from war and went to work "as a peon" on the loading dock of West Publishing Company, Nasseff stopped in to see his boss. He put his hands on the boss's desk, leaned down, and said, "I've got an idea to save this company lots of money. You don't even have to pay me a wage. Just give me a percentage of what I can save you, and I'll be making more than you."

The boss told Nasseff he was pretty cocky.

"If I wasn't, I wouldn't be here."

That boss would become CEO of West, and Nasseff, the brash Lebanese kid from the West Side Flats who never went beyond the ninth grade, quickly became a "respected peon." He would rise to become a partner in the company, and his share in West when the firm was finally sold in 1996 would total a reported $175 million dollars.

And now, in the dapper twilight of his years, if there is a hospital to be built in St. Paul or a dental clinic needed in Lebanon, Nasseff is there. If there is a church to be completed in Minneapolis, a pipe organ to be donated in St. Paul, an orphanage to build in Mexico, or an institution like the Minnesota Club to be rescued, Nasseff is there.

If you've been around St. Paul for any amount of time, you've known or seen John Nasseff because in addition to being one of the city's premier philanthropists, he's a thorough individualist, a colorful one-man style show in a red or black beret who tools around town behind the wheel of a classic Cadillac, an antique Auburn, or one of several silver Mercedes-Benzes.

Nasseff's purchase of the Minnesota Club was recently consummated, and the stately old clubhouse at 317 Washington Street was shut down for a year of long-overdue remodeling.

The only club to which Nasseff has ever belonged will then officially belong to him. (He subsequently sold it to the Minnesota Wild professional hockey team.) The John Nasseff Heart Hospital at United Hospital was also completed this year and is one of the few benevolences that bears his name. He has usually resisted putting his name on his gifts.

"My mother had a saying, 'Allah bahattif,' and that means, 'God knows,'" said Nasseff. "God knows what you do."

Nasseff was only eight or nine years old when he was summoned from his family's home on Eaton Street to meet with Bertha Applebaum, the matriarch of another family that would become famous in St. Paul.

She wanted to see the toughest kid in the neighborhood. Never mind that the Applebaums were Jewish and Johnny Nasseff was Lebanese. This was the West Side Flats. Jews, Arabs, Mexicans, and blacks lived there and got along. Except for Mama Applebaum's Sidney. The bullies were picking on him.

"Why are those dirty collars beating up on my Sidney?" she demanded of Nasseff. "I don't know," he told her.

"Well, every morning I want you to walk Sidney to school and then back home when school is over. And every Friday I'll get you a bag of candy from my Oscar's store."

And every Friday there was a bag of candy from the first Applebaum store at Seventh and St. Peter. Nasseff, who did not pay much attention in school, made another deal with Sidney.

"I copied his homework," said Nasseff. "We got each other through school."

But Nasseff quit school at fourteen, going to work delivering telegrams on his bicycle and stretching leather in a glove factory.

"Twelve dollars a week. My check was for eleven dollars and eighty-eight cents because twelve cents went for Social Security. A guy next to me had been there, stretching leather for fifteen years, for so long that his fingernails curved under his fingers, and he was only making eighteen dollars a week after all those years. I quit to pump gas."

Then Nasseff went away to World War II, serving with the U.S. Army engineers in the South Pacific in such places as Peleliu, Guam, the Philippines, and Okinawa. When he returned from the war in 1945, he had a wife and a child and $240.00 in service separation money.

"That's what was between us and starvation," he recalled. "I got construction jobs as a crane operator, and then I heard they were hiring at West Publishing. I went to work there unloading boxcars for one hundred dollars a month and also drove cab three nights a week. I hated working inside where it was noisy and dirty but loved driving cab. Thank God I didn't quit my job at West."

He talked his way into a deal with his boss, though. He sketched out his plans for changes, some of them were made, and they worked. The company did save money on his ideas, and by the early 1950s he was slowly rising on the ladder behind his first boss, Lee Slater, who would become CEO of West.

"In 1965 a disastrous flood was on the way, and some decisions had to be made to prepare for it. Slater was in Asia, and when the company reached him, he said, 'Nasseff will handle it.' We had hundreds of thousands of books in a warehouse by the river, and I immediately started sandbagging. Then I rented all of the semitrailers and tractors I could find. We got one hundred of them, all moving books and paper twenty-four hours a day. We emptied that warehouse and moved everything to the Midway Stadium parking lot. I had to rebuild the parking lot after that, but we saved the inventory."

After the flood, Nasseff had all the sand from the sandbags on hand, so he rebuilt the warehouse above the floodplain. Along the way, he became warehouse superintendent, then buildings superintendent, then the manager of facilities. Under the leadership of the legendary West leader Dwight Opperman, Nasseff's star at the company continued to rise, and he became part of the inner circle, allowed to purchase stock in the privately owned company. Only key members of the highest echelon were accorded that right, and by the 1980s, John was made a vice president and a member of the board.

"I was also invited to become a member of the Minnesota Club, and that was important to me. When I was ten or twelve years old, we'd come across the Robert Street Bridge—always over the rainbow arches, by the way—and we'd sit on the wall of the public library across Washington Street from the Minnesota Club. We'd watch the big limousines pull up and drop the members off. Then the chauffeurs in their jodhpurs would come over and stand under the trees and yell at us if we'd get too close to their cars. But it used to give me goose bumps just to hear those big old twelve-cylinder cars start up."

In later years, he'd own a fleet of those big old cars, and now John Nasseff owns the club.

He bought the 114-year-old institution in order to save it, he said. Its membership was down, and it lost money five years in a row, largely because some of the corporate memberships, such as those held by its members from West, weren't there anymore.

"I am not a joiner," said Nasseff, "and the Minnesota Club is the only organization I've ever belonged to. That place is very special to me, and I still regret how much it suffered when West was sold. I feel an obligation to try to save it."

West Publishing Company, right across Kellogg Boulevard from the club, was vital to the success of the club, and Nasseff played a key role in the company's 1990 decision to leave the city by 1992.

West needed more office space and Nasseff tried, without success, to negotiate a building permit for land along Kellogg Boulevard where the Science Museum of Minnesota now stands. The city council, however, would not yield to West's request to build above the boulevard siteline, despite Nasseff's public warnings that the company would abandon the city in favor of a new campus in Eagan.

That is exactly what happened in 1992, when West left with its twenty-one hundred employees, more than 5 percent of the total downtown work force. West's decision to leave is still considered one of the worst blows the city took in the twentieth century.

But Nasseff didn't leave. He's chosen to live downtown, less than a half-mile from everything he's ever done in life. In his retirement, he's a colorful, full-fashion fixture—sometimes dressed in a cape that only John Nasseff could wear—at the Downtowner Cafe for breakfast, the St. Paul Hotel for lunch, and Pazzaluna for dinner.

"When I was first in operation here," said Moe Shariff, owner of the Downtowner, "I looked out and saw this man get out of a $150,000 Ferrari. It was red, and he was completely dressed in red: red suit, red shoes, red cap. He looked like a cardinal. That was John."

Moe was also searching for a banker then, when he was still trying to buy his little restaurant. Nasseff said to him, "You have found a banker. When do you need the money?"

He has also bankrolled his personal tailor, an Albanian immigrant in New York City whom Nasseff has installed in the man's own little shop. And every month, Nasseff gets a box of clothing from the tailor; one month it'll be a denim suit, with matching beret, belt, suspenders, shirt, socks, and undershirt; the next month, everything will be in black.

"During my black period," Nasseff joked, "everyone gives me the clergy discount."

And in turn, Nasseff's generosity is instinctive, said former Mayor George Latimer.

"He was always my favorite multimillionaire. His whole life is proof that there is an American dream, that you can really do it."

Mayor Norm Coleman said, "Not for a single waking moment does John Nasseff ever forget where he comes from and where his parents came from. He loves St. Paul to a degree way beyond anyone else I have ever met here.

"He is the American dream for any immigrant kid, and I'm just a huge fan of John Nasseff."

The list of Nasseff's charitable accomplishments becomes more impressive each year. In Bane, Lebanon, his mother's hometown, he built and is maintaining a dental and medical clinic. The new $1 million organ at the Church of St. Louis, King of France, in downtown St. Paul was a gift from John Nasseff and his wife, Helene Houle, in honor of her parents.

He has also built an addition on an orphanage in a small town in Mexico and donated two-thirds of the cost of a $3.5 million expansion project at St. Maron's Maronite Catholic Church in Minneapolis. This gift is made in the name of John's parents.

He is the major donor for the $20.5 million John Nasseff Heart Hospital, described by United Hospital as a "leading-edge cardiovascular care delivery unit." Nasseff, a survivor of a major cardiac crisis himself, was persuaded to allow his name to be used for the facility as encouragement to other potential donors.

"Every day of my life," said Nasseff, "except when I was in the service and when I've been out of town on business or a vacation, I've been in St. Paul. I love this town, and I've said it before: There is a magnetism of the soil. I go back to my old neighborhood, back across the Robert Street Bridge, and walk around the West Side all the time. I am drawn to my neighborhood. And I will not leave it."

<hr>

A Crackerjack Restaurant in a Cracker Box Location

JANUARY 10, 1994

Irv Serlin never needed a key for his restaurant. The mailmen or the trash collector always had the place open, the coffee on, the toaster hot. Irv would get there late, about 5:00 A.M., just in time to garnish the morning coffee with blueberry muffins, fresh juice, Jewish toast, some nice sausage, pie, eggs, a stack of cakes, maybe a couple of pork chops, a slab of bacon, or a side of beef.

"Eat this," Irv would command, piling yet another platter of ambrosia on a cluttered, groaning table way too tiny for all the demands he made of it. "It's good for you."

He said that to the owner of the local Cadillac agency one morning, the coup de grace coming in the form of a melon slice the size of a duck boat topped with fresh fruit and mounds of ice cream.

"I may have once eaten all these things in the course of a single day," said Dick Long, "but never in one meal." It was a feeble, meaningless protest. Long and his companions were dismissed, but only after Irv packed a lunch for them and sent them home with whole pies for their wives.

Serlin's Cafe sits atop the hill on Payne Avenue. There is, there was, not another place like it. A snooty restaurant reviewer from Minneapolis had heard about it once, came over to partake of some earthy Payne Avenue culture, and preceded her column with snide remarks about getting her visa and shot card brought up to date before venturing to the lowly East Side of St. Paul where the natives talk funny.

She missed it entirely, of course. Retired Ramsey County District Judge Archie Gingold could have explained it to her.

"You went to Serlin's to get recharged, and Irv overloaded you. Not only with food, but with his goodwill. He wasn't just serving food. Something else. He was serving an uplift."

Archie Gingold and Irving Serlin were Jewish, but the judge remembered how Irv used to accompany the late U.S. District Judge Ed Devitt to Mass. Irv went to Mass once to mourn one of Devitt's friends, an Irish Catholic priest from St. Louis Church. Irv was profoundly moved, one of the last to leave the church. Such, says Gingold, was his ecumenism.

"No one," said Gingold, was as much an institution in this town as his friend Irv. "No one ever had reason to say an unkind thing about Irv Serlin."

Irv was buried Friday. He died last week at age eighty-one, and from all over people were remembering how the stout, balding cook with bad legs and a tiny kitchen in an outrageously uncomfortable, overcrowded cafe had made their lives so much richer.

"Why don't you make this place bigger?" his friends would wail, their questions made more urgent because they were probably dripping wet from waiting in the rain to get in the front door.

"How many big cars can I drive?" Irv would say. "How many pairs of shoes can I wear? If it got bigger, it wouldn't be Serlin's." And if it were any bigger or more comfortable, he must have known, there were some who would never leave the place.

Former St. Paul newspaper columnist Bill Farmer went to Serlin's before sunup one Thanksgiving morning and found the place with its shades drawn and in almost total darkness. He knocked on the door, and it was opened. By a customer who might have been a U.S. Senator, a mailman, a hockey coach, or state attorney general. As a matter of fact, it was an Applebaum, from the supermarket empire.

"The place was packed with people, and it wasn't even supposed to be open," Farmer recalled. "It was like getting into a speakeasy. The customers were serving coffee and rolls, and Irv was out in his little galley, baking six or eight turkeys to give away for Thanksgiving and fixing breakfast for all these people who just stopped by to see what he was up to. I found a place to sit down, shoehorned myself in, and there's Irv, with juice and blueberry muffins. 'Take, eat,' he said. 'It's good for you.'"

Farmer the newspaper columnist tried to take all this in. A place with eight tiny booths along the side walls, two half-booths the size of ballerina slippers down the middle, and one normal, sane, kitchen-sized table up front for the really lucky. Cartoons on the wall signed by Charles Schulz, Olympic hockey posters signed by Herb Brooks, a photo of Irv on a camel, a photo of the pope, and a sign over the kitchen door that bid "Shalom."

"It was," said Farmer, "one of the most heartwarming Thanksgivings I can remember."

Irv Serlin contented himself with his little cracker box of a restaurant for forty-eight years, borrowing money to open it when he came home from the navy after World War II. He'd been a railroad cook and a troop-train cook, so he was at home in the tiny kitchen in his white T-shirt, apron, and checked cook's trousers. He and his wife, Doris, lived upstairs, and he loved nothing more than to lean out the window and wave to his friends when the Payne Avenue Harvest Festival Parade went up the hill in front of him. The restaurant was all he needed, he'd say, that and a nice, big car and a two-month winter vacation.

"Everyone knew when he'd be open after his vacation," said former Attorney General Warren Spannaus. "On that morning, the line would go clear around the corner."

Spannaus was a seventeen-year-old Rice Street sod layer when he first started going to Serlin's for breakfast before sunrise. He never quit going there, and when Spannaus lost his bid to be governor in 1982, "Irv was more disappointed than I was. I'd promised him he'd get to cook in the governor's mansion."

Irv, should he have wanted to use it, had all the influence that a person could summon. His customers, his friends—his devoted friends—included judges, governors, U.S. Senators, mayors, city council members, and at least one East Side hockey coach.

"All the things you read today about management experts and leadership gurus and lecturers who have the keys to success could be boiled down to one man," said Herb Brooks. "All these people writing books and giving seminars on accomplishment and achievement, they should have hung around this one man. They could have learned so much from Irv Serlin."

Flowers for Elaine

JANUARY 26, 1993

Elaine Furey's last journey was not an easy one. Her friends carried her slowly, haltingly, stopping now and then in the sunny, brittle, cold to rest. Elaine's sister, Leslie Johnson, had walked the icy road earlier in the day, had counted off the steps, because this seemed important to know: It was exactly 380 paces from the front gate to the small place cleared for Elaine on the serene, snowy slope.

Rev. James W. Battle asked for love, for peace, and for Elaine's friends to let her go. Then he gently laid a shovel full of soil in the ground, passing the shovel first to sister Leslie, and then to others who gave their friend the final gift, did one last favor, as taped music softly played "Amazing Grace" and "The Old Rugged Cross." And so the earth received Elaine Margaret Furey on a hill in Oakland Cemetery at the end of Atwater Street.

This is not far from the Flower Hut, a little shop on Rice Street where someone pushed open the back door one afternoon last month, walked in, and, with a hunting knife, put an end to the lives of Elaine, forty-four, and delivery man Al Stafki, seventy-four.

Leslie Johnson and Elaine were a sister act, a team that came to America from Christchurch in the southern island of New Zealand, where their eighty-two-year-old father, Robert Bruce Steele, still climbs down a ladder into the ground to mine gold. Leslie and Elaine would both come to America, Leslie first, in 1965, to New Jersey, to meet the family of the Antarctic meteorologist she'd married.

"I hated America at first," said Leslie. "I didn't want to be here. We got a seven-hundred-dollar phone bill the first month, and the meteorologist ripped the phone off the wall."

She was learning about America. When she first came here, Leslie talked to everyone, the other ladies in the restrooms, the old black man sitting on the curb. You have to understand New Zealanders, who are called Kiwis. Expressions that an American tosses off, such as "See you later," are taken seriously by the Kiwi, who will want to know where and when.

The American says, "We'll get together for a drink," and the Kiwi will show up that night with his family.

New Zealanders are extravagantly social, accommodating, trusting, and Leslie and Elaine were Kiwis to their souls.

Leslie and Elaine had a little flower shop in New Jersey, and when the marriage to the meteorologist went sour, Leslie answered an ad she'd seen about a flower shop for sale in Stillwater, Minnesota. There was a town in New Zealand called Stillwater, quite a lovely place, and when she learned the shop here was near the foot of Myrtle Street, that did it. Leslie's mother's name is Myrtle.

So they all came to Minnesota in April 1984: Leslie, her son, Darrin, and Elaine and her son, Andre.

"I told Elaine she'd love it because everyone here wore baseball caps and union jackets. I trusted the man who sold me the shop. When I asked for a profit-and-loss statement, he said, 'My, you people are formal,' so I didn't insist."

Leslie and Elaine watched themselves go broke in the lovely town of Stillwater. The rent was one thousand dollars a month, and South Pacific Florists was lucky to gross three hundred dollars a week. They knew the end was near when all they had left in the empty shop was the phone, and then it stopped ringing when it got disconnected.

That was the low point, November of that first year in Minnesota. The sister act was down to one car by this time, which then got smacked by a snowplow, so Elaine was hitchhiking up Highway 36 to her new job at a sugar-packaging plant in Roseville. Darrin sold his blood to buy food, and Leslie gathered up all her good jewelry and peddled it to a pawnbroker for seven hundred dollars. This was their America.

With her last two hundred dollars, Leslie put a month's rent down on a little cinderblock building she'd found on Rice Street and Front Avenue in St. Paul. She put together a sign out of scraps of wood and wrote "OPEN" on it. The Flower Hut, more of a walk-in cooler than a real store, was born.

"I sold roses at first for eight dollars and ninety-nine cents a dozen," said Leslie. "When I sold a dozen, I'd take the money and go buy some more flowers."

And because she didn't have a chair, she sat on the stove. To shut her door, she had to chop the ice away with a hammer. Because she didn't have a car, she slept on a sheepskin rug on the floor behind the counter and paid her landlord ten dollars a week to haul groceries to Stillwater. And when she was robbed one day, she had to pay the thieves off in flowers because there wasn't any money in the till.

"I found myself telling the robbers, 'You don't want to take that one, mate, it'll freeze in the cold.'"

But Leslie was selling flowers, quite a lot of flowers, without making any money at her low prices, of course, and becoming an enthusiastic part of her new community.

The Flower Hut, wrote community activist Mike Temali, "appeared out of nowhere, in a tiny, cold, garage-like structure. We all peered in—a family with funny accents was inside, making flower arrangements. How would they ever make it here?"

Temali was then the executive director of North End Area Revitalization, a nonprofit development agency that was trying to reverse decades of business stagnation on Rice Street. Temali and others sensed a new spirit in the Flower Hut, an extraordinary, infectious excitement in Leslie and Elaine that turned the tiny shop into a beacon.

Temali, who would later become a private neighborhood development consultant, worked with Leslie on her plans to expand the Flower Hut. She is, he said, impulsive and "totally midwestern. She gives her flowers away. I don't know how she makes a penny." Temali recalled that his mother and father once received a dozen long-stemmed roses from Leslie with the simple message, "Thanks for giving birth to Mike."

"The Flower Hut helped us imagine the future," Temali wrote in a tribute to Elaine after her death. "They taught us all that we could move into the eighties and nineties without fear of losing our basic feeling of community of being 'Rice Streeters.'"

Leslie, meanwhile, got a five-hundred-dollar Small Business Administration loan through Women Venture of Minnesota to lay in some roses for Valentine's Day in 1985—the first of some welcome breaks. Six hundred square feet of cinderblock store is not a megamall, and when that was bulldozed out from under Leslie, Temali found another location—the old Jack Frost bait shop at Rice and Winnipeg, fourteen-hundred square feet of badly sagging floor space. To Leslie, it was Tiffany's.

Leslie had discovered advertising, and one day a fellow

from a billboard company came in the door. He needed some flowers. How would he like to trade? Leslie asked. Fine, he said, so she loaded him up with roses, her specialty. He gave her a billboard—one with lots of flowers on it. Only they were mums instead of roses.

"I didn't have mums on my signs," she recalled. "I said to him, 'Do you know anything about advertising? Put some roses in!' so he gave me three more billboards, lots of roses, and I became very busy. To this day, I give him a hard time about the mums."

That's how Peter Remes of Midwest Sign became a friend of the Flower Hut. This month, he helped carry Elaine those 380 paces and took the shovel to help bury his friend. On Maryland Avenue, not far from Oakland Cemetery, up near the northern edge of St. Paul, out where the combustible charm and turmoil of the city begins its surrender to suburban calm and refuge, there is now a Remes billboard in simple black and white, an austere announcement that bears the names Elaine M. Furey and Alfred P. Stafki. It says, "We will always remember you. Friends of the Flower Hut."

Leslie was the big sister, four years older than Elaine. Leslie was the emotional one, the dramatic one. She was like a racehorse, high-strung and elegant. Elaine was like the draft horse, the one who just kept cheerfully plugging along in the little store full of flowers and talking birds and a tiny black dog named Abner. Elaine's career at the sugar plant ended after part of a forklift fell on her, breaking her back. So she went to work at the Sears store on Rice Street, showing up to work nights and weekends at the Flower Hut.

Her diversions were Minnesota-simple. She went to Vikings games, with hair painted purple if it suited her, dressed in purple head to toe. The national anthem would make her cry, and she'd sit at home and tape the various renditions that would start ball games, then call Leslie to tell her she had something Leslie must hear. Elaine Furey, and her son, Andre, were in America to stay.

"You got your money's worth at the Flower Hut," said city council member Janice Rettman, "and more. Elaine made you feel that yours was the most important business she had. She was the wind beneath our wings."

Rettman was speaking from the heart at Elaine's extraordinary funeral service at Mount Olivet Baptist Church last month. This is Rev. James Battle's church, a citadel of black culture in the African-American community. And yet it was half-full of New Zealanders and white Americans that day, drawn together out of horror at a crime that had no race, out of affection and love that knows no color.

Mount Olivet was one of two Baptist churches in St. Paul that knew the Flower Hut well. Every Saturday night for the last several years, Leslie has made sure that Mount Olivet and Shiloh Missionary Baptist Church have donated flowers for their Sunday services.

"Leslie and Elaine came to help celebrate my twenty-fifth anniversary in the ministry," Battle said. "They didn't just send flowers. They were here. When we dedicated our new fellowship hall last February, Leslie was here. She spoke."

Battle was there for Leslie. When the bodies of Elaine and Alfred Stafki were discovered, the family sent for Battle. "I knew they needed me. I was asked to go in, and I thank God that he had me ready. This family has brought something out of the tragedy. They brought all people together, black, white, Hispanic, the churched, and un-churched. Before they went back to New Zealand, Leslie's family helped me celebrate my birthday at my house, and they don't realize it, but they were ministering to me at that point."

Battle is a leader in St. Paul's Ecumenical Alliance of Congregations, and he became a liaison with the press following the Flower Hut tragedy. It was Battle who had early contact with the man who ultimately would confess to this crime. Two days after the bodies were discovered, a man called and told Battle he could carry the guilt no longer and wanted to know if God would forgive him.

"I told him God hated the sin but loved the sinner," said Battle. "And I waited for him to call back."

The man who called Battle later turned himself in at the VA Medical Center at Fort Snelling. Charles Ray Wilson said in his confession that he succumbed to demons inside him when he plunged his knife into Elaine and Alfred, and he is being held without bail, indicted by a Ramsey County grand jury on four counts of first-degree murder.

Mike Temali remembers that awful day in December when he was called to the Flower Hut. Leslie's son, Darrin, and another friend, Rice Streeter Rob Linder, were cleaning up after the crime. Temali was not sure he could walk through that door, so heavy was the feeling of loss and dread in him.

"I walk in, and there's Rob and Darrin, working, and Jimmy, the black bird next to the counter, says, 'How are you?'

"How am I? I'm crushed! I'm destroyed!

"But Rob Linder goes, 'I'm fine. How are you?' Obviously, he wasn't fine, but he said he was. It snapped me back. It said to me that we have to go on. If the man who was there cleaning the carpet after such a crime can go on, we can go on. I think of Elaine and what she would have said."

Elaine Margaret Furey would have said, "Good on ya, Mate!"

A Laidback Little Old Waterfront Shanty

MAY 22, 1999

You can't buy a bowl of booya there anymore, nor one of those sinfully good chilidogs, and the man in charge probably won't tell you your walleye or northern is an eelpout. But Tally's Dockside will take you back in time, more than half a century in time, to the White Bear Lake's la-de-da resort era.

Now in its sixtieth year, Tally's is one of the very few places left in the Twin Cities where you can still rent a fishing boat for the day. Surrounded by the glamour of a robust community, Tally's is still the same little laid-back waterfront shanty where generations of lake lovers have come for bait, a boat, and a bite to eat.

Tally's occupies just 150 feet of shoreline in the westernmost bay of the lake and is tucked between two thriving marinas full of sail and power boats. When Clarence Elsner, the original owner, built his rustic little cabin in 1939 and called it the Anchor Inn, U.S. 61, the main road between the Twin Cities and Duluth, ran right alongside the lake.

"Some of our customers came out on the bus," recalled Esther Elsner, widow of Clarence's son, Marlin. Marlin and Esther lived in a former gas station that had been converted to a cafe-saloon directly across the highway from the boat docks.

She remembered how busy the little place was. Clarence had a dozen wooden boats built at the Amundson Boat Works next door, right over by the Plantation Ballroom (also long gone). Boats then rented for thirty-five cents per hour or two dollars for the entire day.

"Clarence built that building all by himself," said Esther, "and even though they added on through the years, the basic cabin is still the same."

By 1942, the Elsners sold it to the next owners, and eventually it would become the property of Mildred (Millie) and Ralph (Tally) Blommer, who changed the name to Tally's.

"My husband loved to play cards when he was a little kid," said Millie, "and he picked up his nickname from the tallying of points. It stuck, I guess."

Tally is remembered as a jovial, fun-loving entrepreneur who loved to make booya in forty- and fifty-gallon batches to serve to his customers. Booya, three-two beer, and chili dogs. I remember boating from the other end of the lake many times for one of those dogs, and in later years, long after the Blommers had gone, Millie's secret recipe had been replaced with factory-made Hormel out of a can. It was still a Tally's chili dog, though, and I would have rowed across the lake for one.

"Tally had a great sense of humor," his widow recalled. "He loved to have fun with the boaters. If they came in with a big walleye or a northern but didn't know what it was, he'd tell them they'd caught an eelpout. He didn't know what an eelpout was, but it sounded good."

Tally suffered a stroke in 1979, however, and had to sell the business (he died six years later). After a couple of more owners had operated the place, it caught the eye of a young couple who had come here from Madison, Wisconsin. Keith and Jan Dehnert were running a water ski shop across the street. (U.S. 61 has long since been moved farther inland, and the old highway is now a one-way street that passes between Tally's and the historic Johnson Boat Works.)

"My wife and I are former water skiers with the Tommy Bartlett show in the Wisconsin Dells," said Keith. "We did that from 1978 to 1985, but then we graduated from college (University of Wisconsin at Madison) and had to get into the real world.

"Somebody told me the best place in the world was White Bear, so we came here and opened the shop. And I would look across the street at Tally's and wish that I had that business."

Keith finally did buy it, in 1991, and made important but subtle improvements that did not alter the historic feel of the picturesque little shanty. By then, requirements in local health codes had pretty much ruled out such delicacies as booya and chili dogs being served out of a boat shack, and Tally's today is more of a convenience store (with catering available) than a four-star restaurant.

Boat and pontoon rentals are still available, though the rate for a metal fourteen-foot boat and motor is a little more than two dollars a day (more like fifty dollars to seventy dollars, depending on which day). Pontoons rent for $180 for six hours, and Keith suggests reserving them two weeks ahead.

Tally's is open seven days a week, Monday through Friday from 8:00 A.M. to dark and Saturday and Sunday from 6:00 A.M. to dark.

This year, for the first time, Tally's is getting into the marina business itself, with new docks and forty slips for pontoons and power boats. Each slip will rent for one thousand dollars for the season. That may seem steep, but Keith said, "We even have a waiting list."

That's another thing has not changed at Tally's over the years. Business is still very, very good.

Leaving "The Hustle" Behind

SEPTEMBER 27, 1997

It was probably just one of those impulsive little jewelry heists. A customer in the pawnshop apparently saw something he couldn't possibly do without, so he grabbed the flashy, expensive necklace off a display and headed for the front door. The culprit and his loot were just twenty steps from freedom.

A young clerk, being an alert sort, saw all this and quietly told pawnbroker Bob Peltier what was happening; a three-thousand-dollar gold choker was rapidly going down the twenty steps from the second-floor pawnshop to the entrance on Grand Avenue.

Bob soared into action and threw the heavy electronic bolt on the front door. The top door that separated the jewelry man from the pawnshop also has an electronic lock because there is absolutely nothing that the pawnbroker has not been through in this business.

"I called the police, and after a while they came," said Bob in his deep, "Victory at Sea" voice. "Didn't matter, though, because this guy wasn't going anywhere. I looked though the bulletproof glass at the top of the stairs and waved to the guy at the bottom of the steps. He was wondering what to do, and he finally stuffed the necklace into the mailbox.

"The cops came, I opened the bottom door, and there this man was, all by himself, going, 'Who, me?' They didn't have to ask who the thief was, and they clamped him in cuffs, put him in the car, came back with the video camera, and got footage of me slowly turning the key in the mailbox, opening it, and then taking out my heavy gold necklace. The idiot should have gotten a year and a day just for being stupid."

Bob, sixty-two, has been the loquacious proprietor of Viking Pawnbrokers and Jewelers on Grand Avenue for thirteen years and is, at the end of the year, retiring from "the hustle." He has, he said, his health and "ten percent of my sanity." And he's grown weary of dealing with his "silent partner"—the City of St. Paul.

His license to operate a pawnshop cost him $876 in 1994. In 1995, it rose to $2,500 a year—a reflection, city licensing personnel say, of the effort required to regulate and police the city's ten pawnshops. While business license fees generally increase 4 to 5 percent per year, the jump for the pawnshop fee was 285 percent.

The city may be able to justify that huge increase in fees, but Bob now has other things to occupy his time.

Boxing, for one. Bob's basso profundo was made for the ring, and in the last six years he has done a fair amount of announcing for amateur and professional fights. His dream is to work nationally as a ring announcer.

"It's all show business," he said. "That's all part of the hustle."

He has been in on the hustle since he was a kid, growing up on St. Anthony between Albert and Pascal and attending Central High School. His practical education included driving a taxicab and bootlegging booze out of the trunk during an era when it was never necessary to go thirsty in St. Paul at any hour of the day or night as long as the right color cab was in the neighborhood.

He drove a semi-truck over-the-road, was a roustabout with Royal American Shows, and worked with the highway department for eight years. He even worked at a downtown strip joint once, where it was his job to blindfold the horse so it could be led upstairs for the big show.

You could say that Viking Bob is no beginner. I asked if he was married.

"We did that three times. I'm my attorney's longest living client, and he informs me that if he sees my name on other than a pawnshop license, he'll have me committed."

When Bob finally did get into the pawnshop business years ago, he stayed because "I enjoy the hustle. Once in a while you hit it big on something."

Or get hit yourself. In March 1986, two armed men came into a pawnshop he previously operated elsewhere on Grand Avenue. One of the men began scooping up rings from a jewelry counter while his partner tried to put handcuffs on Bob. The fellow had trouble with the cuffs, so he momentarily laid down the long-barreled pistol he'd been holding tight up against Bob's skull.

That gave Bob just enough time to pull a gun of his own that he had tucked in his waistband. His first shot caught the would-be robber over the eye.

The wounded robber then got his shot off, hitting Bob and bringing the pawnbroker's lifetime total of accumulated bullet holes to four. The fracas spilled over into the street, with the robbers fleeing and Bob right behind them, blasting away with his gun. He recovered, and the thieves were caught, tried, and convicted.

To this day, Bob is never too far from a weapon. The .38 caliber Smith & Wesson he produces from somewhere under his shirt is a serious little handgun loaded with large silver-tipped bullets.

"For werewolves," he growled.

There are some Peltierian rules that will be in force until Bob's departure. One sign in the shop reads, "We take NO checks for NO reason from NO body." Another sign announces, "Walls bullet-proof. Windows bullet-proof."

Bob says pawnshops are unfairly characterized as being hotbeds of stolen merchandise. Of five thousand Viking transactions last year, he said, only six were found to involve goods that were not honestly come upon by his customers.

He also grouses about the computer he has been forced to get to meet the city's new electronic reporting procedure for pawnshops. Until just recently, pawnshops sent copies of pawn tickets to the city's pawnshop investigators so that pawned goods could be manually scanned for stolen property.

(St. Paul licensing director Bob Kessler said pawnshops are being encouraged to participate in the automated system. For those who do, the license fees will gradually be adjusted downward, he said.)

There's still a $1.50 per-transaction fee for the reporting that the pawnbroker has to pay, plus the capital outlay for the computer and software that he has to maintain. Standard interest rates on pawned goods, however, are 30 percent per month and usury laws do not apply to pawnshops. People in this business do not have to suffer.

"I may eventually get back into something without all this bureaucratic involvement," said Viking Bob.

"Ninety-nine percent of the people who come in here come by this place for legitimate reasons. They're living close to the edge and then blow a tire on the car, so they come in and pawn something so they can get to work until pay day.

"One percent are idiots," Bob added. He prides himself with being able to spot the idiots. One guy came in once with a handful of white gold jewelry.

"Now, white gold was popular in the Forties and the Fifties. This guy was too young to own any of that. I took it in pawn anyhow, and after he left, I called the pawnshop sergeant. They put the description of the jewelry out, and it turned out it had all been taken in a Roseville residential hit in which an eighty-four-year-old woman was beaten.

"The thief was identified from my videotape, and he was arrested, charged, convicted, and plea-bargained his way down to twenty years. That guy was bad, and I helped put him away!"

Lt. Richard Iffert, a thirty-year veteran of the St. Paul Police Department, is supervisor of the vice and pawnshop unit. Bob, Iffert said, "is a stand-up guy. We've been grateful for his help many times (in tracing stolen goods). He just has a great deal of integrity."

In another crime situation, Bob served as an expert witness for the prosecution in a murder trial in which he was called to the stand to evaluate jewelry that was important evidence. He was asked to don rubber gloves before touching the goods, and one of the gloves split wide open as he was sliding it over his hand. Ramsey County District Judge Lawrence Cohen remembered the scene well.

"Watching him was like watching someone out of a Damon Runyon story, and his testimony was the most interesting thing in that sad, sad trial," Cohen recalled. "He just about brought the whole courtroom down in laughter when the glove split.

"Bob looked at me," Cohen said, "rolled his eyes and asked, 'Low bidder?'"

St. Nick

FEBRUARY 25, 2000

The conversation between patient and doctor went like this: "Just how good are you, Doc?"

"I've been doing this for a lot of years, Nick."

"Well, if you get this one right, you won't have to pay for a steak for the rest of your life."

Nick Mancini laughed quietly when he told of that introduction to his heart surgeon. Nick looked like the statue of Abe Lincoln, sitting there in an easy chair in his living room, and the top end of the new pink railroad track down his chest was peeking over the collar of his blue robe. His sad, sad eyes looked just a bit sadder, and he kept apologizing for his low voice. His throat was sore, he was tired, and he hurt. That seemed weird to Nick, because any other time he was away from the restaurant for even a couple of days he couldn't wait to get back. This time, he didn't know when he'd return to work. Work, for maybe the first time in half a century, was not his primary thought.

"Jesus, that was a tough operation. I can't get my strength back. But tell that doc to come and get some steak." Nick has poured his life, his soul, into his famous Mancini's Char House on West Seventh Street in St. Paul, and when he recently underwent triple bypass surgery at United Hospital, he learned just how popular he is and how important he is to his town.

The hospital was deluged with an estimated seventy to eighty bunches of flowers for Nick, and he received many hundreds of cards and other get-well wishes. Some of the cards were stuffed into long boxes on a coffee table in Nick's living room.

"I had to put a receptionist on the phone to read a press release to all the people who called to find out how Nick was doing," said Nick's son, Pat. Pat and another son, John, are Nick's partners at the restaurant. Nick and his wife, Mary Ann, have two other children, Gina and Nick Jr., who are not in the business.

Ironically, less than a month after Nick's triple bypass surgery, Mary Ann underwent triple bypass surgery herself. Nick then spent several hours each day at the hospital, visiting Mary Ann and undergoing outpatient rehabilitation himself.

"I've been at the restaurant for twenty-five years," said Pat, "and I don't know everyone who comes in, but every table you go by, someone asks, 'How's Nick?' It's just hard to imagine how deeply he touches everyone he meets in here."

"In every good and kind sense of the word, Nick is the

benevolent and generous godfather of West Seventh Street," said Nick's physician, Dr. Tim Rumsey (with permission from Nick to speak about his patient). "I was at Dave Cossetta's restaurant down the street one day, and Nick came in and started buying pizza for everyone. I already had mine, so he gave me three dollars."

Nick's generosity comes from his eagerness to please. After decades of enormous success in the restaurant business, he still seems baffled by it and in perpetual fear that everything he has may all somehow go away.

"You usually have to wait here to be seated," said Pat. "If Nick sees someone leave because they get tired of waiting, he'll go out on the street and drag them back in."

Nick Mancini was born seventy-five years ago on the Upper Levee, one of St. Paul's Italian neighborhoods that has been lost to progress. The Upper Levee was on the Mississippi River west of the Chestnut Street–Shepard Road intersection, and Nick and all the levee kids used to swim in the river right under the High Bridge. The Mancini family moved off the levee up to McBoal Street right after an older sister drowned in the river when she was thirteen. Nick was six.

"But I still hung around on the levee. I hung around on West Seventh, and I hung around over on the East Side with my cousins. I was an altar boy at Holy Redeemer, I'd go over to St. Ambrose, the Neighborhood House, to the Badlands (a long-gone residential area where Regions Hospital now is). I knew everyone in the Badlands: La Nasa, the Azzones . . ."

Nick went to Jefferson Elementary School and Monroe High School, where he did not excel. His savior was the famous Professor Norton, the principal who went out of his way to help Nick graduate in 1946.

"I needed one credit to graduate, but I only lasted one week in Latin. He put me in typing then, and the teacher told Norton, 'He ain't going to last here, either.' So he put me in cooking class. That I could do, and I graduated."

Nick spent a couple of years in the army in Japan and came

home with a nine-hundred-dollar bankroll. He considered several business opportunities but took the advice of his sister Bertha and bought a three-two beer bar on West Seventh Street. That was the Kato Bar, where Nick served Kato beer, a strange-tasting concoction brewed in Mankato.

"I've known Nick for fifty-five years," said Jim O'Hara, executive director of the state boxing board (who has since died). "My wife's Uncle John was a retired blacksmith out on Seventh, and he went into Nick's place every day for a nickel glass of Kato beer. Nick raised it to a dime, and Uncle John started going to another joint down the street.

"This worried Nick. He asked me where John was, and I told him. Nick says, 'Tell him to come back and I'll sell him beer for a nickel, but not to tell anyone else.'

"And that's how he built his bar business. A nickel at a time."

O'Hara also recalled that Nick wanted to be a ball player, so he sponsored a baseball team at Palace Playground. "Everyone knew that Nick was not exactly Mary Poppins on his feet, but he dragged me out to Palace one day with a keg of beer and all the bats and balls. He told the coach he was there to play first base. The coach said he already had a first baseman. Nick said if he couldn't play first, he'd take his bats, balls, and beer and go home.

"He played first base, but he was no first baseman."

O'Hara was always active in boxing, as a boxer and an official.

"Nick also wanted to be a referee, but I knew he was about as good a referee as he was a first baseman. I told him I'd only let him in the ring if he had boxing shoes on. Nick's got size sixteen feet, so I knew he'd never be able to find shoes. He didn't ref."

But Nick found his forte in the bar business. It agreed with him, it made sense to him. He sold his mother's spaghetti for sixty cents a plate, and by 1949 he had added pizza. He also knew that he needed to sell liquor as well as three-two (allegedly non-intoxicating) beer. So he and a pal, Bud Faricy, went to the post office in 1956, where Nick bought a liquor license. On their way back to Mancini's, they stopped at the old Jackson Buffet to see a pal, Al Unise, who gave them a jug of Cabin Still.

"We took that back to Nick's place, and he opened it up and poured me his first shot of whiskey. He just kept moving up, remodeling and expanding."

Nick eventually decided to go into the steak business on a pizza-and-hamburger street. The first night he served two dinners. He had more staff than customers, and one night three guys came in and Nick thought he was in heaven. "How's your steak?" he asked one diner.

"'How's my steak? It's burned! This is the worst steak I ever had! Fire the cook!'

"So Nick went back and told the cook. The cook told Nick the guys were drunk and they were no good and he should throw them out.

"Now my cook wants to throw the only customers I got out of the joint," said Nick. "He had a big fork in his hand, and I had all I could do to keep him from going after them. But what do you say to your cousin?"

His cousin, the late Perry Cucchiarella, did not kill the customers that night and eventually, in a couple of years, the steak business grew. Nick has expanded five times, and you could safely say that he and his sons are among the most successful restaurateurs in Minnesota.

On any Friday or Saturday night, Mancini's will serve nine hundred to one thousand steaks. Any other night of the week is a five-hundred- to six-hundred-steak night. His two-hundred-car parking lot is perpetually full. His weekly meat bill, exclusive of lobster, is forty thousand dollars, and Nick still examines every steak that is served to make sure it is up to his exacting standards.

"He's plenty sharp," said O'Hara, who is in the produce business. "I've done business with him since 1968, and no one pays on time like Nick. His word is as good as gold. He's a soft touch but sharp." His longtime adviser and distant cousin, the late majordomo Frank Marzitelli, once said, "The secret of his success is this: Where else can you go where the owner visits with all the patrons and not just a few? He genuinely wants everyone to have a good time."

"He goes on vacation and he hates it," said another pal, Pat McCarthy. "He went to Italy once with Dave Cossetta, and his long-distance phone bill was greater than the airfare. He can't stand to be away from the business."

He does go to Las Vegas now and then. One time he brought with him a box of frozen walleye for an old friend and former bartender, Tony Geisbauer, who was by then a Las Vegas vice squad cop.

"It was 110 in the shade, and Nick is lugging this box of fish all over town," recalled Don Del Fiacco, a retired *Pioneer Press* columnist and close friend. "He goes into the Tropicana, and the pit boss asks him, 'What's in the box?' Nick says, 'Fish,' and the pit boss says, 'Eat 'em, dump them, or let them play blackjack.'

"We went to Caesar's Palace, and the fish are getting ripe. Nick lays them on the baccarat table, and everyone is shocked and dismayed."

"I finally found a casino where they knew Tony," said Nick. "I asked for Tony Geisbauer, and they said, 'You mean Mr. G?' He got his fish."

There's a scrappy side to Nick as well. Back in the days when a well-known boxer went by the name of "Boom Boom" Mancini, Nick got mad at a fellow restaurant owner and dropped him with a single pop in the nose. Some of Nick's friends had a jacket made up for him with printing on the back that said "Boom Mancini."

One time Nick got involved in a brawl in his parking lot and wound up testifying in Ramsey County District Court on the force that police used to subdue an allegedly unruly professional hockey player. Nick took a police nightstick and began rapping it on the railing of the witness stand to demonstrate how hard the cops were beating on the hockey player. He whacked the railing so hard the end of the nightstick broke off and sailed into the jury box, narrowly missing a juror.

But it will be Nick's generosity, and not his fisticuffs, that he will be remembered for, said an old buddy from the Badlands, Joe Azzone.

"I've been in to see Nick, and he'll toss me the keys to his car and ask me to take a big box of food out to a house on Watson or Armstrong.

"I'll ask him, 'Who lives there?' and Nick will say, 'I don't know, but I hear the guy's out of work.'"

A couple of years ago Nick called Connie Perozino, who lives in the Windsor Commons high-rise next door to his Char House.

"How many people you got over there?" Nick wanted to know.

"One hundred and twenty units," Connie said.

"Bring them over for lunch."

"All of them?"

"All of them."

"It was like a parade of the elderly," she said. "Nick gave us a beautiful lunch, he played the accordion, and he sang 'I Did It My Way.' He had so much fun he did it again for everyone at Christmastime. He's a peach of a guy."

Other restaurants seem to change decor and cuisine with the seasons, but Nick's place stays the same. You want steak? He's got steak. You want lobster? He's got it. Salad. Walleye. Baked potato. You want artichoke hearts and filet of hummingbird tongue? Go somewhere else.

Many of his customers come just to watch Nick patrol his huge shop, long arms flapping in the breeze as he barks out orders to bring some wine to this table, some birthday cake to that one, some wings and sausage to the one over there. He issues gift certificates for two steak dinners to his friends, who seem to be everyone in the place. When Nick is really happy, he goes onstage and sings "I Did It My Way."

"You put ads in the newspaper if you need more customers," said Nick. "I don't need any more customers, but what really helps is that personal contact, the hospitality thing. I always want to give something back to my customers, to make them happy."

So when he was in United Hospital recently, right after he had undergone bypass surgery, Nick threw a Super Bowl party. He had Dave Cossetta haul in a half-dozen pizzas and big buckets of mostaccioli and a case of wine, just for the hospital staff and anyone else who happened to be passing by.

And when he was ready to leave the hospital, Nick phoned his son, John, to come and get him.

"Bring forty gift certificates when you come," said Nick.

A Real Grocery Store

DECEMBER 8, 1993

How do you pack 115 years into cardboard boxes? Just how do you take down and fold up a legend? Can you walk away? That's what excites, yet troubles, Phil Kormann right now; his retirement winds it up for his family after three lifetimes in one grocery store, three generations of Kormanns on a little corner of Railroad Island.

Kormann's store at Burr and Minnehaha on the East Side henceforth will be run by someone other than a Kormann. The new owner is most recently from Chicago, and while the building will still bear the name, the Kormann family will be out of the business that has occupied it since grandfather Anton came from Bavaria in the 1870s.

There may be no other grocery store in the state with such a long, one-family history of ownership. Anton was first, with his original store at University and Lafayette. And then came Phil's father, who spent his life in the store that has been on Burr Street since 1886.

Phil the elder originally didn't want to be a shopkeeper, but that's exactly what he was, and when Phil the younger was making plans for his career, dentistry seemed infinitely more exciting than sacking potatoes and sugar in the basement of the family store.

"I considered it menial duty, not a very glamorous business," said Phil. "But after two years of dentistry school, I was back in the grocery business. Down through the years, I've decided I was much happier as a grocer than I would have been as a dentist."

The whole thing is like interviewing George Bailey from *It's a Wonderful Life*. Phil Kormann, in the way he walks, talks, moves his hands, is Jimmy Stewart, with his lanky, tweedy, Main Street enthusiasm and innocence. Phil, in his gentle, courtly way, radiates the casual courtesy of a genuinely kind man.

He's been meaning to look up a poem his father used to recite about shopkeepers that began, "If I possessed a shopper's store, I'd drive the grouches from the floor; I'd treat each one who came to buy . . . " Phil doesn't remember the rest, but he knows just what the guy meant.

Kormann's is so old that it was there before the Italians got to Swede Hollow. Back in the early days, a fellow named Mel Roth had a little store on Whitall and Burr. Later, Roth would become president of the Red Owl grocery store chain, and he would start the Shopper's City empire.

Those operations are gone now. And Kormann's little store remains.

Joe Tucci was the longtime butcher who made Italian sausage from an old family recipe, sausage so popular that the store sold two thousand pounds of it one week. Joe retired a couple of years ago, and then Betty Searles, Kormann's head cashier for twenty-two years, retired in 1992.

It wasn't the same without Joe and Betty, and Phil began to look to his own retirement after fifty-two years in the store. He and his wife, Jan, have three children, but they all have different career plans.

"There's a grieving process you go through when something like this comes to an end," said Phil. "But I think I'm through it. Now I'm going to try to think of the rest of that poem."

<hr>

An Airport in Plane Peril

SEPTEMBER 24, 1993

John Benson, operations director, security chief, and food and beverage manager at Benson's International Airport, had a way of dealing with such calamities as aircraft-controller strikes. Just keep circling to the left, John advised his pilots, and every once in a while, holler out.

Benson's International Airport, perhaps the tiniest independent airport left in the Twin Cities, is on a hill across Highway 61 from Bald Eagle Lake. It still awaits the arrival of the Concorde. If it comes, its landing will be delayed if there's a pig roast on the runway.

Under John Benson, all important milestones in aviation, such as the month of June, were celebrated with a pig roast. And if someone soloed, or married, or showed up on a Saturday night to see what was going on at the hangar, there'd be a party at Benson's International.

Last week, two hundred friends and fellow fliers gathered there to celebrate the life of John, who died recently of cancer at the age of seventy-one. This was not a wake but another big hangar party, and he would have heartily approved. At his birthday just last month, John, fully aware of his limited future, read a poem he'd written, one that ended like this:

". . . So now, with not much left to save or spend,
What's more important, you have lots of friends."

In a corner of the hangar this week, a table full of gray-haired pilots toyed with a model of John's favorite plane, the J-three Piper Cub, a plane that was a perfect match for the man because of its simple, honest, durable, and gadget-free dependability. The pilots all grew up near Benson's International.

"We were sophomores in high school, and we flew from here in one of John's planes out to Withrow to chase cows," said Al Lindholm. "Think of it. When you're a sophomore, you can hardly get the family car."

Another flier, Ross Sublett, said, "There are no fences at Benson's. If you were a kid on a bicycle and rode up and watched the planes fly for a while, chances are pretty good you'd get up for a ride. That's the kind of place this is."

The airport is the last sixty acres of the old Benson family farmstead, with its two-thousand-foot grass runway right next to the two-pig roaster and the big, round, above-ground swimming pool that looks like a Mongolian yurt. The shortness of the runway, pilots say, makes for more resourceful fliers. It also keeps the big stuff away. The landing lights are forty-watt bulbs, which replaced the construction markers swiped from Ramsey County years ago. And parked under two rows of precarious-looking shelters are the single-engine Cubs, the Stinsons, the Aeroncas, the silver Luscombe, and the gliders for which Benson's is home.

Benson's International Airport is a relic, an artifact from less-official, less-regulated times. But it lies in the path of progress, and John's friends will likely have to fight to keep it operating.

"There is nothing else like this. Not anywhere," said flier Dave Black. "There was a hangar, the grass strip—and there was John."

Healing and Serving

A Palace Full of Children

JULY 16, 1994

While I was growing up on the West End of St. Paul, I'd often go up the hill to my grandfather's home in Highland Park, right across Warwick Street from the mysterious, big, red-brick palace full of young children. Whoever lived in that castle, I thought, had to be the luckiest kids in the world. They had horses to ride and orchards, stone barns, and huge fields to play in.

At about the same time, one of the kids who lived in that castle was looking out of her world. How lucky the kids were on the outside, Paula Gonzalez thought. They actually had real homes to live in, with their mothers and fathers right there with them.

"I'd look across the street and think, 'Oh, gee, if only I could be there,'" Paula recalled, almost five decades later. She lived at St. Joseph's Orphanage at Randolph and Warwick from 1941 to 1949, along with her two sisters and brother. More than thirty-five hundred children would live at "St. Joe's" in an era when the orphanage was the only refuge for children from bad, broken, or no homes.

Many non-Catholic children lived there over a period of years, and many children who were not even orphans. There were children whose mothers were sick with TB, with cancer, and whose fathers could not care for them. The Gonzalez kids were not orphans. Their mother had died, and their father went away to World War II, leaving them in the care of the orphanage.

"It was the only home I knew," said Paula. "I went there when I was only one and a half years old, and I called the nuns 'Mommy.'"

There was Sister Evangeline, after whom Paula would name her daughter, and Sister Marsha, who taught first grade at St. Joe's and was "really sweet." There was Sister Mercedes, a tiny, dark-haired woman, and Sister Mabel, the nun who "I got my lickings from. She was tough."

The Sisters of St. Benedict cared for orphaned and neglected children of St. Paul for 112 years at St. Joseph's Orphanages in both St. Paul and in south Minneapolis. In 1994, the Catholic Charities honored the sisters for their work, which had its roots with the Assumption parish in 1869 as the "direct result of the vicissitudes of pioneer life, several Indian massacres, the Civil War, and epidemics which deprived children of parental care," according to a history of the orphanages written by Sister Claire Lynch, the first principal of Archbishop Brady High School.

The need in St. Paul increased as the orphanage outgrew several smaller downtown locations, and St. Joseph's in Highland Park was completed on a forty-seven-acre tract of open land in 1900, a tract it would later share with Cretin High School. The orphanage was a baronial five-story fortress with a high gabled front decorated with dormers, blind arcades, and a squat central pinnacle atop which was a modest cross. A wide concrete stairway led to the columned portico at second-floor level, giving the structure an aura of invulnerability and dour fortitude. The building was the epitome of nineteenth-century institutional severity.

"It was just like a palace to me," said Dorothy Hodges of Inver Grove Heights, who went to live there in 1940 with her five brothers and sisters when the marriage of their parents dissolved. Dorothy would live at St. Joseph's until she was eleven, about the maximum age for children at the home.

Dorothy never felt that she was missing anything in life, not even her own special day. Everyone's birthday was celebrated on the same day, and there'd be a cupcake on each dinner plate along with one nickel.

"The orphanage taught us how to work, how to worship. It taught us discipline, and for my brothers and sisters and me, it was for the best at the time. When I'd tell my children about how tough things could be in the orphanage, they'd roll their eyes and say things just aren't like that in the modern world."

Girls and boys were segregated in the building, sleeping on different floors, playing in separate play areas, working at their chores apart, and even eating at different ends of the dining hall. Paula said she and her sisters got to see their brother, Victor, only in passing at mealtime.

Playrooms, classrooms, dining rooms, the chapel, the nuns' living quarters, and the girls' dormitory occupied the lower floors, and the boys' dormitory was in the attic, or the fifth floor, in a space that was bleak and barren. During thunderstorms, the sisters would get the boys out of bed and have them kneel in a circle around a lighted candle to pray the Rosary, which was an unforgettable experience, some children recalled. And the sisters, ever frugal, would keep the wax that dripped from the candles, melt it, and the children would use it to wax the floors.

The population at the home went as high as 283 children in 1923, and sisters literally operated the place on a shoestring—the annual operating budget never exceeded thirty-six thousand dollars—because most of the food was raised or grown in the fields surrounding the orphanage. Vegetables picked in summer and fall were canned or buried in wet sand and used all winter.

"We'd go out in the fields and pick corn, tomatoes, onions and dig potatoes," Paula recalled. "We had an orchard and always had a big box of apples in our classrooms. Whenever we went out for recess, we had to eat at least three apples. Sometimes they'd be a little shriveled up, but we ate as many as we were told to eat."

The orphanage raised chickens and even had a dairy herd until the early 1930s, when the neighbors began complaining about livestock noise and odors. A team of cart-pulling ponies given as a gift, however, was kept at the orphanage for many years.

The sister orphanage in south Minneapolis operated much

the same way, and two of the inhabitants of that institution were brothers Frank and Pat Marcogliese, who are now in their eighties and live in St. Paul. When they were children living on the Levee in St. Paul, their mother became ill and was hospitalized at St. Peter. Their father could not care for them, so they wound up in the Minneapolis orphanage.

Pat was only six years old and recalled that, even at that age, he was expected to help in the fields by pulling weeds or picking bugs off potato plants. When the orphanage's chickens were laying, the kids each got one Sunday morning egg, hard-boiled. But usually the morning meal was "mush," Pat remembered.

"The nuns would lick you if you didn't eat the mush, but I couldn't eat it and wouldn't eat it, so I got licked. Finally, they got tired of licking me and let me alone. I was a terrible kid, just awful, and I deserved every single licking I got."

The routine was much the same in St. Paul, Paula said. Oatmeal (into which was mixed cod liver oil) for breakfast all year long, and maybe once or twice a year the kids got an egg.

"This sounds strange, but I was happy when I was there," said Paula. "And I didn't want to leave. It was my home, and once, after our father came home from war, we did leave for a short time, but because where we lived wasn't so nice, we went back to the orphanage.

"We didn't think we were missing out on too much by being in an orphanage. We actually had more opportunities than other kids to go places and see things. We went to Highland pool to swim, we went on picnics, to Excelsior amusement park. We went to see Gene Autry once, and to the Ice Capades. We really had it all, much more than if we had not been there."

When she was eleven years old, Paula was released from the orphanage and went to live with her father permanently. She wanted to go to a Catholic school, but he couldn't afford to send her there, so she went to a public school, where she felt lost and confused. The adjustment for Paula was long and difficult.

At its busiest, almost three hundred children lived at the orphanage, but by 1960, only fifty-four children were left there. Society by then had found alternatives to orphanages as long-term refuges for children. Foster homes were becoming more popular.

There'd also been a fire at St. Joseph's Orphanage in 1955, and the city came down hard on several hazards that would have been extremely expensive to correct. The decision was made to close the institution, and the building that had been home to more than thirty-five hundred children was demolished in 1960. An apartment building and Derham Hall High School were built on the land.

Years later, Paula's last name would become Murphy, and marriage would change Dorothy's last name from Auge to Hodges, and the two girls who grew up together in an orphanage would go to high school together. They now work together at the Gillette Company in St. Paul.

"I only wish that the building would still be there," said Dorothy, "so that I could have shown it to my children. The only thing that makes me sorry about where I grew up is that it's no longer there."

Windows into a Hospital's Past

MARCH 3, 1998

The corridor in the old photo is dark and gloomy, seems endless, and is occupied by a solitary man hunched over on one of the wooden-slat park benches that made this a waiting room.

The photo brought me back to the times I waited there years ago for my friend Rudy, who got knocked senseless in a football game; for a girl named Kathy, who tobogganed into a tree; and for a cheerleader named Sandy, who was injured in a car wreck.

This was Ancker Hospital in St. Paul, and this corridor was where you waited on old park benches while urgent and mysterious things went on in the emergency room. This is where Ramsey County judges sent juvenile traffic offenders on Friday and Saturday nights to record what they saw and how they felt when the ambulance cases came screaming through.

Rudy, by the way, went on to become a high school principal, and Kathy married a newspaper reporter who became a columnist. Sandy died of her terrible injuries at old Ancker Hospital.

This ancient photo that brought so much of it back for me is part of a dramatic new exhibit at Regions Hospital, a "Living Wall," according to Marketing Vice President Annette Wagener, that ties together 125 years of St. Paul hospital history.

These showcases outside the hospital's main-floor cafeteria are permanent windows into the hospital's past, back to the old nineteenth-century stone mansion run as a hospital by Dr. Jacob Stewart, a prominent physician and three-term mayor of St. Paul.

Back in the 1860s, St. Paul was a river town, with numerous brothels and more than 240 saloons, so injuries and casualties were common, along with diseases such as diphtheria, typhoid fever, smallpox, and tuberculosis.

The ten-room Stewart mansion was purchased and established as the county hospital in 1873 under the leadership of Dr. Arthur B. Ancker, who, it can be said, started small: A sixteen-by-sixteen-foot room served as a reception and examination room, sleeping apartment for the two staff physicians, a storeroom, drug room, dispensary, and general office where all the books were kept.

But under Ancker's guidance, the hospital by 1913 had become the nation's tenth-largest hospital and the biggest west of Chicago. Ancker pioneered ambulance service, beginning with a two-horse carriage run out of a garage that doubled as a morgue and a mortuary.

Ancker also established a nursing school in 1891, and the

Living Wall memorializes what a physician told graduating nurses on commencement day in 1907. Your business, he said, "first, last, and all the time is to be neat, to make friends of the patients, to learn their idiosyncrasies, and to cook dainty food."

But Ancker also led the way in caring for tuberculosis patients, in the development of catheterization techniques, and heart surgery, and by the early 1950s, it was clear that the bustling old hospital and its many additions needed to be replaced.

Ancker was situated alongside an equally busy railroad track on the West End, where the St. Paul school district offices are located today. The old "Short Line" railroad crossing at West Seventh Street seemed always to be occupied by a train when an ambulance had to get to the hospital. No one knows how many babies were born and how many seriously ill or injured people died waiting for the track to clear and how many ghastly train-car wrecks occurred there, but pleas for a grade separation went unheeded, ironically, until after the hospital moved to its new location east of the State Capitol.

The old Ancker identity went out of the place when it became St. Paul-Ramsey Hospital with that move in 1965, and even though the facility has changed its name twice since then—to St. Paul-Ramsey Medical Center and, most recently, to Regions—there are old die-hards in town who still refer to the place as Ancker.

The owners of Regions, HealthPartners, have invested seventy million dollars in building and system upgrades and are determined that the new name, connoting a lofty new mission, will eventually be embraced and understood in the community.

This new exhibit is a gallant recognition of the institution's past. While I was looking at it one day, several staff members and patients came by, looked, and muttered, "I remember that," or "I was in that ward, I was in the burn tank."

"We literally rummaged around in our attic to find these

artifacts," said Annette Wagener. "Luckily, through the move in 1965, so much was kept in box after box. And when the call went out for historical items, employees and old patients brought things in to us."

The wall's designer, Rick Cucci, also credited the Minnesota Historical Society and its collection of Ancker photos and artifacts. The project was a challenge to him because there was so much material and relatively little space for its display.

"What was particularly gratifying to me was that while we were putting the display together, so many people came by and thanked us just for remembering."

One of those who remembered was Bev Johnson, an operating room nurse who recently retired. Bev goes back to the days of an old hospital by the Short Line.

Bev brought a gift from her personal archives, a gift that is now a prominent part of the Living Wall: a surgery towel, with blue-on-white printing that boldly says, "Ancker Hospital."

The Preventorium

JUNE 21, 1992

The youngest kids at the Preve thought everyone grew up that way. Didn't everyone sleep on a sun porch all winter? Didn't all kids get to pick their Christmas presents out of the Monkey Ward's catalog? Didn't everyone have a horse named Skipper to ride, and didn't every kid have to swallow a spoonful of castor oil each morning?

The Preve was where a timid little boy called "Eggbert" from Como Lake cut a willow switch and became a musketeer, where he quickly learned to pick the hottest soapstone off the cookstove to keep his bed warm through a long winter night on the porch.

The Preve taught Eggbert to swim, and he became the captain of his own shipwrecks. It gave Eggbert a bathrobe, and he spread it on the floor and turned it into a chariot for races in the dining hall.

The Preve was isolation, but such splendid isolation: a cool, rural fantasyland on a lakeshore out Rice Street.

The business of the Preve, the Children's Preventorium of Ramsey County, was to care for children who were at the brink of tuberculosis and to give them health. The Preve (rhymes with leave) also gave the children community, camaraderie, and security. There was good food and, when they needed it, warmth. No one was poor at the Preve, even during the Depression, so when the time finally came to go home— after one thousand days or even three thousand days—some children weren't really eager to join the poverty of the real world. The place wasn't a hospital; it wasn't a prison; it wasn't an orphanage. It wasn't really a school, and it certainly wasn't home. It was . . . the Preve.

"Going there was scary," said Winifred (Oldenburg) Stanek. "At ten years of age, you want to be home with Mom and Dad. But it was not entirely unpleasant; they had ponies, and swimming, and a little school there. At Christmas, we could ask for anything we wanted. I got a guitar . . . "

Young Wini Oldenburg lived at the Preve for a year. She was . . . what? A resident? A patient? An inmate? Now, fifty, sixty, and seventy years later, those who lived at that peculiar place really don't know themselves what they were because, at the time, they didn't realize they were very special children at a very special place.

"As a kid, who knew different?" asked Father John T. Brown, a Cannon Falls priest who went to the Preve when he was five in the mid-1920s. "I was not aware of any other way of life. I had never seen a dog until I got out there."

Stanek and Brown were among the more than one thousand children aged five to sixteen who lived at the Children's Preventorium, an institution that had but one mission in its nearly forty-year lifespan: to prevent the spread of tuberculosis, known then as the "white death." Tuberculosis in the 1880s caused one out of seven deaths in this country. Even into the 1930s, it was the leading cause of death in Minnesota among communicable diseases.

The Preventorium was established in 1915 on the shores of Lake Owasso in what is now Shoreview, on the site of the Cuenca Sanatorium, which had been built to treat those unfortunates that society called "consumptives." Guided by Dr. Henry Longstreet Taylor, the emphasis shifted from treatment to prevention, particularly among children who'd been exposed to TB or had the "tendencies" to develop it. Taylor was the Mother Teresa of TB treatment, pushing obdurate old politicians into the realization that those who had TB, or who'd been exposed to it, must be treated rather than shunned.

"He made enemies," one biography of Taylor reads, "arousing the antipathy of several physicians by his insistency on the necessity of public care of those afflicted."

Taylor knew what those kids needed. They needed good food and rest—up to eleven hours of sleep a day. They needed cod liver oil, so they lined up for a spoonful of it each morning, just before they had their temperatures and pulses taken. They needed sunlight, so they lay outside in rows in "sunboxes" when the weather was right and under "Alpine" lamps indoors during the winter, while their teachers read to them about Darkest Africa and Nancy Drew. They needed fresh, cool air, so boys and girls alike played outdoors in diapers called "drapes."

And every night of the year, except for the most bitterly cold nights, the children would sleep on screened porches, unheated except for three-gallon crockery "pigs" of hot water and stove-heated blocks of soapstone that would be wrapped in newspaper and tucked into their beds next to them.

"We'd push our beds out of the warm dorm into the cool dorm every night, and that's where we slept, summer and winter," recalled Clara Franklin, who was Clara Kalischko then. No one ever froze to death, Clara and other Preve alumni say, and everyone had warm blankets and fuzzy nightgowns. But the kids woke up many mornings and had to brush snow off their beds. Clara went to live at the Preventorium in 1933 when she was eleven years old because her brother had developed TB.

"I really wanted to go there because we were poor. I never got a present before I went there, and one Christmas I got a pair of skates. A snowsuit another year."

People who are otherwise unfamiliar with the Preventorium might remember one thing: photos of young boys and girls, some of them almost teen-agers, romping around in snow wearing nothing but skimpy white diapers. The photos taken in those days leave the impression that the children actually lived outdoors all winter.

"We'd go out in our little diapers," Clara remembered. "But we wouldn't stay out. Miss Loretta Flaherty was the boys' nurse. She'd go out every morning, all winter long, and put her finger in the air to check the cold. Her finger told her exactly how long we could stay out, and then she'd pass the word along, whether it was going to be five minutes or ten minutes."

But in warm weather, recalled Bob Schabert, a retired *Pioneer Press* sports writer who was at the Preve from 1927 to 1935, "we were outside all day long." Schabert got the nickname "Jingle Bells" because one cold winter night the other boys in his porch dormitory heard muffled singing. When the covers of his bed were pulled back, Schabert was curled up around his soapstone, singing "Jingle Bells" to himself.

The cluster of red-brick buildings that comprised the Preve is gone now despite the heroic efforts to save the campus made through the years by persons like Del Meath, who served as a counselor at the Lake Owasso Residence for mentally retarded adults, the facility that replaced the Preve.

One of the artifacts that Meath discovered was a big ledger book that contained the names and brief biographies of all

1,035 children who lived at the Preve from 1915 to 1953. The ledger is four decades of history, recorded one child at a time as it happened. First comes the name of the youth, the admission date, the parents' names, and nationalities. Then the weight of the child and a brief medical history. Some notations read, "Scarlet Fever" or "Diptheria." On across the ledger's wide pages moves the story of each youngster. It tells the length of stay, in days, and the reason for leaving. "Wanted at home" was a common reason, as was "Father removed child." Less common was "Ran away." Even less common: "Deceased."

The daily routine for the healthy seldom varied: lots of sunshine, lots of rest coupled with vigorous exercise (often led or coached by young adults who were former Preve residents), and cool, fresh air. Everyone wore the uniform, those diaperlike drapes, in order to get full exposure to the sun and air. When the girls began to mature, they exercised apart from the boys.

Gerald Dexter, a St. Paul police officer, lived at the Preve and can remember that boys and girls were strictly segregated.

"The boys even had one nurse who would warn us against having any contact with the 'ginks,' which was her word for girls. We went to class and church together and ate together, but there was no other contact with the girls."

One of those girls, Theresa Allie Weber, remembered "they encouraged you to be tough. You were not expected to cry or feel sorry for yourself. You learned to be brave about the little bumps and bruises."

Theresa's mother was Vina Allie of St. Paul, and ten of Vina's thirteen sons and daughters lived at the Preve at one time or another. Sending them there never got any easier, Vina said, but added, "What else was there to do? Where else was there to go? They might have died." Vina's husband had developed TB and was in old Ancker Hospital several times for stays of up to three years. So her children, as many as four at a time, went off to the Preventorium.

Theresa, who was at the Preve for three years, said, "None

of us cared to go to the Preve. Some of us clung to our mother and didn't want to leave the car once we were there. But it made it easier because some of our sisters and brothers were there. And once we were there, we lived the good life. We ate well, went swimming and fishing, rode horseback . . . "

Children could go home only for a week each summer. Their parents could drive out from town to visit on Sundays or take the trolley car to Rice Street and Maryland and hike the rest of the way. Once a week, the kids at the Preve could cross the old Soo Line tracks and go to Guerin's Grocery Store to spend their pennies on candy.

They could also fish, and the staff would clean and cook their catch for them. They could garden, and the staff would prepare the vegetables in a salad for them. They didn't have to go to the circus; the circuses and the Winter Carnival came to them. Time at the Preve was, in many ways, one endless summer.

"To this day," said Gerald Dexter, "people think you're from another planet when you tell them how you grew up."

The Preventorium, throughout its existence, was only marginally supported by tax dollars. It was inaugurated with a donation by railroad magnate James J. Hill, and it was supported through the years primarily with the sale of Christmas Seals from the Tuberculosis Association. In the early days, the Preve operated for more than a year on a total budget of less than eight thousand dollars—much less than the cost of the average one-week hospital stay for just one person today.

And the Preve did turn out some robust young specimens. Photos from bygone eras are of trim, tanned youths of both sexes dressed like Tarzan.

"We'd wait until a storm would come up over the lake," recalled one Preve resident, Fred Quass, "and then take the rowboat out into the choppy water and play 'man overboard.' The nurses would be watching from shore, tearing their hair out. But no one ever drowned. We couldn't drown! We swam every day at the Preve. We were like fish!"

But did the treatment at the Preve work? Mary Usenik, who served as Ramsey County nurse from 1949 to 1982, said the Preventorium "was considered a success. In the mid-1950s, surgery and drugs changed the threat of TB. But before that, when I started working, all we could offer was either bed rest or a collapsed lung."

The Preve's medical success was only part of the story, Usenik said. A kind of rugged individualism was also practiced there, the same kind preached by a man who left the mainstream many years earlier to tend to his health and mental well-being in an eastern wilderness existence lesser people might have perceived as cold and Spartan.

His name was Thoreau, Usenik recalled, and he survived because he wrapped himself in a Preve of his own making.

Volunteering among the Vets

NOVEMBER 11, 1995

Being an angel of mercy in a hospital full of veterans gets to be an adventure. Florine Larson was pushing an old geezer down the hall in his wheelchair once when he slowly ogled her out of the eye that wasn't covered with a patch.

"I get two hundred and forty-seven dollars a month, and I need a wife," he announced. "Are you married?"

Yes, said Florine. But thanks anyhow.

"That was a few years back. I didn't have the heart to tell the sweet old boy two hundred and forty-seven dollars a month wouldn't go very far even then."

Florine winked, giggled, and got into another story about one of her vets at the Veterans Administration Medical Center in Minneapolis, this one about the old fellow from Wisconsin who wouldn't eat, wouldn't talk, wouldn't get out of his bed. The hospital was on the verge of sending him to the psychiatric ward when a volunteer from the American Legion asked Florine if she'd try to draw him out, maybe coax a few words out of him.

Draw him out! This is the party who could have coaxed a soliloquy from Calvin Coolidge. Florine had the Wisconsin vet up to the TV room and ready to eat in record time.

"I just told him about all the muskies I used to catch up at Manitowish Waters, and that got him going. I knew that no man from Wisconsin could stand being out-muskie-fished by a woman."

Florine doesn't do all this for a living, for a paycheck. She's a volunteer who makes her way via bus or cab from her home in Golden Valley to the VA Center to donate a full eight-hour shift each Thursday. That's a good three days' march from the VA Center, and she's missed only a few shifts in the last forty-five years.

"Know what?" she said. "The newspapers always print pictures of someone very important putting flowers on veterans' tombs on Veterans Day. That doesn't do anything for those vets because they're dead. The vets who matter to me are the ones who are still alive."

Nobody would argue with Florine. At eighty-two—a remarkably young eighty-two—she's earned the right to a few opinions.

"My boss, the director of volunteer services, fires me about once a month," she said. "I make him hire me back at double my salary. If that was real money we're talking about, they'd owe me the national debt."

Her boss, Steve Moynihan, directs about eighteen hundred volunteers at the huge VA facility, the flagship of the national veterans hospital system, which was opened in 1988 to replace the sprawling old hospital that dated to the 1930s. Florine does stand out, Moynihan admits, because of her warmth, her sense of humor, her ability to connect with any patient, and because nobody has been around as long as she has.

"You know why they built a new hospital?" she asked. "I wore the old one out."

Most of Florine's 16,845 volunteer hours have been clocked in the chemotherapy ward and among cancer patients. I asked Florine how she can keep her sense of humor among such pathos.

"Would it do them any good if I was crabby?

"One time, I walked up behind an American Indian who'd had brain surgery. He had a big scar all around the top of his shaved head. I ran my finger over the scar and said, 'Hmmm. Now we're scalping the Indians.'"

The woman with the Helga-style braid across her head has a Maurice Chevalier twinkle in her eye and a mischievous laugh, but she's not one to be trifled with. A panhandler sidled up to her at a Minneapolis bus stop, a move that would have terrified most eighty-two-year-olds.

"I said, 'You know, a man your age should be ashamed trying to beg money off an old lady like me!'"

Which leads her to another story. She was talking to a group once about her experiences as a defense plant worker during World War II. A young woman said she couldn't understand the big fuss over that war, which, after all, was "just another war."

"Another old lady asked me what I did during the war and I said I sewed parachutes. She said 'My son was a paratrooper. Thank you!'"

Florine's respect and admiration for vets goes back to three brothers who fought in World War II and her first husband, who was a veteran of the China-Burma theater. Her son, Joseph, is a veteran of the Korean War. Her career as a volunteer—she also works in a nursing home each Monday—goes back to the 1940s.

"My 'real' job was in sewing dresses, and I did that part time. A boss once said to me, 'Why don't you quit that other silliness at the hospital and work here full time?' I told him, 'I'll quit here before I quit there,' and I did."

That reminds her of another story, this one about the woman who was visiting her husband when Florine walked by.

"Do you remember Florine?" the wife asked.

"Of course I do!" the old vet snapped. "I'm sick, not dead!"

(Florine Larson's incredibly long run as an angel of mercy to the patients at the VA medical facility ended, volunteer director Steve Moynihan said, when she died a few years ago.)

A Clinic's Final Hour

MARCH 30, 1994

From the State High School Hockey Tournament to the emergency room of Midway Hospital is quite a bounce, but there we were. Son Erik was on a gurney, still in his breezers and shoulder pads, his face about the color of his at-home jersey. A doctor we didn't know popped in to say Erik's shattered kidney had to be removed. Now.

Call someone, Erik said to me. Find out what's happening. Then a friend was with us, Erik's doctor, our doctor. "At ease, Erik," said Dr. Kenneth Lerdahl. "We took a longer look. You'll keep your kidney."

That was three years ago, and Erik has long since recovered. But you remember those moments with your doctor after thirty years of childhood sicknesses, athletic injuries, and the various infirmities of life that prompt those frantic phone calls in the night.

I remember him also for some surgery we performed together, with me supplying the skin and Dr. Lerdahl doing the sewing. We were going neck and neck in at-home klutziness both times, and when I came in one day after running a channel iron through my leg, the doctor had just fallen out of an apple tree.

"This will be my first left-handed operation," he said. A

few years later, I'd sheared the end of a finger off and went to Lerdahl for some stitchery.

"This will be my second left-handed operation," he said. "I just tangled with a power saw."

Recently, our family was among the thousands of patients in the Twin Cities who got letters that said "Please be advised that after having served the Midway community for over a century, Midway Family Physicians regrettably will be closing for business April 15."

Dr. Lerdahl's small family clinic is not closing because it wants to. It is closing because it is a small family clinic that has to. It is closing for many of the same reasons that Divine Redeemer Hospital in South St. Paul closed, because medicine has become such a colossal, complex business that huge blocks of patients are traded around the insurance industry like home mortgages around the banking fraternity. Who's your doctor? What month is this?

Dr. Lerdahl was in his office last week, and for once I got to see him without rolling up my left sleeve. He talked about his thirty-three years of practicing medicine in St. Paul.

It's all about managed competition now, he said, about corporate concepts and controlled care for consumers.

"We used to call them patients," Lerdahl mused. The clinic is growing more quiet the closer it gets to closing, and each day some of the thousands of soon-to-be former patients call or come in. The younger ones want their records, and the older ones just want their doctor. Dr. Lerdahl, sixty, will practice somewhere, and many want to go wherever that is.

Having a family clinic was a big deal in the 1970s, and next month this place closes like the mom-and-pop grocery store that lies in the shadow of a supermarket.

This closing business is like a death, Dr. Lerdahl is finding. He knows the stages well. This is, he advised, the final hour.

War Veterans

Trip to Pearl Harbor

NOVEMBER 10, 1991

It was Sunday morning, and Ensign Guy Flanagan was dressing for the usual in-port weekend routine. He put on his khakis and his wristwatch, and he got into his shoes just in time to watch his ship die.

Fifty years ago next month, the battleship USS *Arizona* was parked in a neat row along with seven other American battleships at Pearl Harbor, even as 423 Japanese airplanes were picking the Hawaiian islands out of the Pacific mist. The first wave of the attack broke low over Ford Island at 7:40 A.M. Ensign Flanagan began the sprint to his battle station in the bowels of Turret No. 3 as soon as "general quarters" was piped from the quarterdeck.

He slid down a ladder leading to a passageway between the ship's after turrets. The ship was a few hundred yards aft of battleship USS *West Virginia* and shielded by the moored repair ship *Vestal*, so it escaped the first torpedoes that were slamming into the other battleships—but not the pinpoint onslaught of the Japanese dive bombers.

One of the bombs dropped right down the *Arizona*'s smokestack, exploding a boiler and a forward ammunition magazine. A Japanese pilot later recalled, "A shock like an earthquake went right through our formation, and my aircraft shuddered with the force of it. It was the *Arizona* going up."

Flanagan was jolted by the hit, the lights in the passageway went out, and the air was filled with a nauseating gas. Somehow Flanagan found the door to the turret's powder room, through which he could escape, but it was secured from the inside. He was soon joined by other crewmen as he beat on the door with his fists; in desperation, he rapped out an SOS with his wristwatch, at the same time praying aloud to be let in. So hard was his banging that his wrist was cut and his watch shattered. So urgent were his prayers that he became known to survivors as "Father Flanagan."

They were let in, but the powder room was only a temporary refuge. The men could not raise the plotting room on the ship's battle circuit or even the turret itself by sound-powered telephone. The room was dark, filling up with fumes and water in its lower reaches, so Ensign Flanagan and another officer ordered the men to higher decks inside the turret: to the electrical deck and the shell room and finally to the pits of the turret itself. Flanagan ordered the men to stuff their shirts in telescope ports to keep the fumes out as the ruined ship continued to settle in the water. The turret crew was long gone from its position, and finally Flanagan's survivors opened a door from the turret and escaped onto the *Arizona*'s quarterdeck, which was being periodically raked with machine-gun fire.

When he got on deck, Flanagan could watch the destruction of his ship. It seemed to be ablaze from the boat deck forward, and he unleashed the life raft for Turret No. 3, ordered enlisted men into it, and shoved it off through the water. Then he helped load wounded onto the admiral's barge and left with it to take them to the relative safety of Ford Island.

He looked back once, and his ship was ablaze from his turret to the bow. He didn't know it then, but more men were killed on his ship that day than on any other ship in naval history. The USS *Arizona* lost 1,177 men the morning of December 7, 1941—almost half of the men who died that day at Pearl Harbor. By the time the attack was over at 9:45 A.M., there were only 337 survivors of the *Arizona*, among them the twenty-three-year-old ensign from Mankato, Minnesota.

"I didn't know him before the war," said Flanagan's wife, Merry. "But before we were married, he told me about that day aboard the *Arizona*. He said, 'There. That's it. Now, I won't ever talk about it again.'"

I talked to Merry a few days ago in the family room of their Roseville home. There are shelves on one wall filled with the mementoes of Guy's war: his medals and decorations, a model of the *Arizona* as she looked before that day, and a small model of the Pearl Harbor Memorial that is built athwart the sunken battleship.

After Pearl Harbor, Guy recuperated from lung damage he suffered breathing the *Arizona*'s smoke and fumes. He joined the war in the Pacific, at one point commanding a seagoing tug that had to tow a damaged destroyer through a typhoon, for which Lieutenant Commander Guy Flanagan received a personal commendation from Admiral Chester Nimitz.

Pearl Harbor and the *Arizona* did not beckon to Guy until well after the war. Merry says he did not talk about his war experiences until after they visited the memorial for the first time in 1981.

"There were some tears shed," she recalled, "and then he could talk about it. That was a catharsis of some sort."

Since then, they've been back to Hawaii twice, and they planned to return next month for the fiftieth anniversary of the attack on Pearl Harbor. Guy, seventy-three, a retired state employment officer, had gradually become an active member of the *Arizona* survivors crew.

This year, as its chaplain, he'd planned to take part in the memorial service on December 7. Guy and Merry had bought their airline tickets and made hotel reservations. He was the only survivor from his living compartment on the *Arizona,* and the most profound event of his life had become very important as life itself was nearing an end.

As I talked with Merry, Guy was at home, suffering from terminal heart disease in its final stages. He did not have the strength, nor the time, to attend the memorial service, and he died on November 19, 1991.

But he had made arrangements for his burial, from the memorial built atop his battleship. As a privilege afforded only to its survivors, Guy Flanagan had his ashes scattered on the water that laps at Turret No. 3, his battle station, the last visible sign of USS *Arizona.*

Still Living "A Day of Infamy"

DECEMBER 7, 2001

Sixty years ago this morning, Robert O. Carlson, Sr., was tuning up his saxophone, getting ready to play the national anthem at morning colors on the fantail of a battleship parked at Pearl Harbor.

Carlson and his shipmates were just twelve minutes away from the sinking of their ship, the USS *Oklahoma.*

At the same time, seaman Don Keis was coming topside aboard his battleship, the USS *Maryland,* tied up to the port side of the *Oklahoma.* He arrived on deck as the first attacking Japanese plane made its pass less than two hundred feet overhead.

"It was so close I could see the pilot. He was looking at me, and I was looking at him."

U.S. Army Private Platt B. Walker was a couple of miles away from Battleship Row that morning, at Fort Kamehameha, near the entrance to Pearl Harbor. It was 7:55 A.M., and Walker was back in his tent after going out to get a Sunday newspaper. He heard the bombs strike Hickam Field nearby and lifted the flap of the tent to look out.

"In the sky," Walker wrote in a guest column for the *Pioneer Press* in 1990, "beyond the first clouds of smoke came lines of aircraft, dozens of them, coming down from the distant mountaintops to the northeast. They were in beautiful string formation, line upon line of them as far as the eye could see.

"They clearly had the red ball of Japan's rising sun on their wings. Not dozens, but hundreds of aircraft."

Carlson, Keis, and Walker are all Minnesota survivors of the Japanese attack on Pearl Harbor six decades ago today. They are in their eighties now, but their memories are vivid of the day when more than twenty-four hundred sailors, marines, and soldiers lost their lives there.

These survivors all have one other thing in common: They recall how absolutely unprepared the military was for the attack.

"We weren't at all ready for it," said Keis, a retired employee of the *Pioneer Press* who lives in St. Paul.

"All of the small arms and the ammunition were locked up, the officers had the keys, and most of those guys were ashore."

And at old "Fort Kam," Private Walker kicked in the door of the ammunition locker after his supply sergeant, who was drunk, refused to give him the keys without an order from the commanding officer.

The soldiers on the ground that day fought the Japanese Zeros, Vals, and Kate aircraft, the Kates loaded with seventeen-hundred-pound torpedoes, with World War I bolt-action Springfield rifles.

"I also had a World War I thirty-caliber water-cooled Browning machine gun with tripod," wrote Walker, who lives in St. Paul. "Two fellows hustled it out to where we could see skyward."

Machine-gun fire also was coming from the attacking aircraft, and the fort was raked again and again.

Each time, the Americans dived under barracks and other buildings until the attack passed.

"Once our guys had loaded guns and ammunition in hand," Walker recalled, "fear began to subside. An intense calm seemed to set in—a profound alertness. We had clear shooting. Wind was carrying the immense black smoke to the north. Japan's planes were now attacking from the south, where they could see targets. And they were our targets.

" 'Lead 'em,' someone said. 'It's just like shooting ducks and geese!' And so it was for a hunter. It felt the same. But now we were shooting at men. Strangely enough, a sort of quiet animation, good spirits, sharp humor began to set in. Later, I realized that this warm rapport was our first taste of the camaraderie that men feel when fighting for their lives together in battle."

Back aboard the *Oklahoma,* Musician First Class Carlson was watching the planes coming in when the first of several bombs and torpedoes sliced into his ship. He was on his way to his battle station where he was assigned as a lookout on the superstructure.

He never got there because by 8:08 that day the *Oklahoma* had completely turned over at a cost of 429 lives, second only to the 1,177 men lost when the battleship *Arizona* was sunk.

"I went into the water on the port side," Carlson said, "and was taken aboard the *Maryland.*"

After the attack was over, pounding from the inside of the hull of the *Oklahoma* could be heard, and Carlson helped cut holes in the bottom of the ship. Thirty-two sailors were rescued through the hull.

"The USS *Oklahoma* took seven torpedoes for us," recalled Don Keis. "We got one torpedo, one bomb hit us, and we were strafed by machine gun in the second wave of the attack. But the smoke coming from the battleships *Tennessee* and *West Virginia* obscured us. We got lucky."

Of the seven battleships parked next to Ford Island, four were lost: the *Arizona, California, Oklahoma,* and *West Virginia.* Only one, the USS *Nevada,* got under way during the attack but was hit by five bombs and subsequently beached off Hospital Point by its skipper to avoid blocking the main channel.

Don Keis would go on to serve on several destroyers in major battles in the Pacific, including the Battle of Leyte Gulf. He was discharged as a boatswain's mate at the end of the war.

"I saw a lot of war," he said. "But I loved those destroyers."

On December 8, Private Walker became a sergeant without ever being a corporal. He went on to fight in Okinawa, leading his men ashore under fire. When he came home in 1945, he was discharged as a first master sergeant, the highest rank a non-commissioned officer could then make.

Musician Carlson, meanwhile, earned a commission and

was trained as a pilot. He made a career of the navy and retired as a lieutenant commander in 1964.

"You know," said Carlson, "When I joined the navy in 1939, I was a lousy student and just not ready to study at college. I had to grow up first. Twenty-five and one-half years later, I had been to several colleges in the navy and wound up doing just exactly what I loved, what I enjoyed."

Carlson has served as state chairman of the Minnesota Pearl Harbor Survivors Association, which numbers 111 men, the youngest of whom is seventy-eight years old.

The survivors association includes members of the crew of the USS *Ward,* a destroyer manned primarily by naval reservists from Minnesota and the ship that fired the first American shot of World War II just outside Pearl Harbor when it destroyed a miniature Japanese submarine.

To commemorate this date, members of that survivors association each received a sixtieth anniversary gold ring from Jostens, the Bloomington-based jewelry company that has crafted more than fifty million rings for high schools, colleges, military academies, and sports championships since it was founded in 1897.

"This sixtieth anniversary is the last one the association will celebrate in Honolulu," said Carlson. "But the Minnesota chapter will continue to observe the date at the Fort Snelling Chapel.

"We'll never stop doing that until the last man is gone."

Bataan Death March Survivor

JANUARY 23, 1991

It's branded into his skin, into his mind, something he'll never be free of, said Bernard FitzPatrick. A half-century after he tried to leave it all in another world, the Bataan Death

March comes back to take his sleep. The worst part for him is the thought that right now, somewhere in a Middle East desert, young soldiers are being prepared for their hell.

"I hate to listen to or see the war news," said FitzPatrick. "It turns my stomach to think that for some young guy, his ordeal, like mine, might just be starting."

Bernard T. FitzPatrick was a young graduate of the College of St. Thomas in 1941 when an unlucky draft number sent him to the 194th Tank Battalion. He wound up on the island of Luzon in the Philippines, and World War II was just a few hours old when the Japanese army began pushing seventy thousand underfed and under-equipped Filipino and American soldiers toward the small end of a thirty-mile-long peninsula known as Bataan.

After Bataan fell in April 1942, FitzPatrick began his nineday, 104-mile walk in the sun. Of the ten thousand Americans who began the forced march to Camp O'Donnell in the interior of Luzon, two thousand died en route. Another twenty-three hundred would die in prison camps during the next three months. Only eleven hundred lived to see the end of the war, and fewer than three hundred are alive today.

The march settled into a grisly pattern. The weakest and the sickest would buckle and fall and be bayoneted by the Japanese guards. A few fortunate ones, FitzPatrick said, were shot.

"I hated the system," said FitzPatrick, "but I understood it. The Japanese officers were just as brutal to their own soldiers who were weak."

Life at the end of the march did not improve. If one prisoner at the camp escaped, ten men were chosen at random and shot. FitzPatrick said a fellow captive had to stand at attention and watch his own brother get executed. After he was shipped as a prisoner to Japan when the war was crawling to its conclusion, FitzPatrick and other survivors of Bataan were put to work in a steel plant.

When American bombers came over in waves, he shared

bomb craters and ditches with the civilians, and when the bombs set off firestorms, even the handmade Japanese wooden dog tags the prisoners wore would ignite.

In 1945 he came home, having survived malaria, beriberi, jungle rot, pellagra, dysentery, deafness, vision loss, and the Bataan Death March. During the last fifteen years, FitzPatrick has poured his experiences into the manuscript for a book titled, "The Hike," which he hopes to see published soon.

"I can account for about ten percent of why I managed to make it," FitzPatrick said. "The other ninety percent is a mystery or perhaps the result of my mother's prayers. I do know I am living proof that I am not here entirely of my own efforts."

A WAVE Yeoman

APRIL 14, 1993

The U.S. Navy now wants to put women in front-line combat jobs. The mission is to quarter women aboard our warships, to send them to sea in submarines, and to make fighter-plane pilots of them.

That's a significant departure from the early days of the women's navy, when World War II WAVES automatically became storekeepers, nurses, and paper-shuffling yeomen. WAVES of that era were governed more by what they couldn't do than by what they could.

They couldn't go to sea, they couldn't advance beyond the rank of captain, and they couldn't dress like male sailors. Women in the navy, above all, couldn't get pregnant. If they did, they—and not the fathers—were history.

Mickey Remitz of Forest Lake was among the first to volunteer in 1942 for the new women's branch organized to free up men for combat duty. Mickey became a WAVE yeoman and spent her three years in the navy at the Great Lakes Naval

Training Center. Mickey is unabashedly proud of her naval career and fiercely loyal to today's navy. I asked how she would have reacted to a combat assignment.

"Why not? You have to remember that in 1942, we'd just been attacked by the enemy, and the reason everyone enlisted is we were all very angry and wanted to fight. I told my bunkmate, 'If they'd give me a gun, I'd go over and shoot at those guys.'"

Mickey and another WAVES, in fact, volunteered to shoot training rifles.

"We were both from Minnesota, had been hunters, and figured, 'Why not us?' We wanted to prove we could do it, and we both got marksman badges. We didn't have to do that, but we did."

Mickey also regrets not touring a submarine when she had the chance. It was her only chance to go aboard a real naval ship, and I asked if she'd have volunteered for sea duty, or even combat flight duty, had it been possible.

"You bet. We were pretty patriotic and would have done anything. I would love to have been a pilot. I would love to have gone to sea. But you know how it is: Those darn guys get everything . . ."

Marjorie Beane of St. Paul joined the WAVES in 1943 and became a dental technician through schooling so accelerated that she's still amazed at how much she learned in such a short time. The navy taught her that given the opportunity, and the challenge, she could do anything.

"It taught me that women are just as good as men. If the individual is qualified to be a pilot or to be aboard a fighting ship, then they ought to get the job."

That would have been a radical thought in 1943, and Mickey and Marjorie had to be content with roles that supported the male navy, but for both of them, it also meant lifetime alumni membership in a pretty exclusive club.

Now the navy is changing, due in part to its battered image in the wake of the Tailhook scandal and pressures put on all branches of the military by the issue of homosexuals in service.

Two old salts named Marjorie and Mickey will have to miss the boat. They were born just fifty years too soon.

Explosion in the South Pacific

SEPTEMBER 11, 1999

When the men of the USS *Mindanao* reunite in St. Paul next week, they'll remember the worst day they have ever known, a November day almost fifty-five years ago in a crowded wartime harbor in the South Pacific.

The *Mindanao,* a repair ship, started that day anchored near the USS *Mount Hood* in Seeadler Harbor of Manus Island in the Admiralty Group. This was a huge harbor, capable of berthing more than six hundred ships.

But of all the other 271 vessels anchored there on November 10, 1944, the *Mindanao* was closest to the *Mount Hood,* an ammunition ship that was conducting loading and unloading operations. That meant one-hundred- to five-hundred-pound bombs were being pushed around and rolled up and down ramps only 350 yards away.

"Nobody was too eager to be alongside that ship," Bill Ryan of Maplewood recalled. "We were anchored at the bow, and at times the sterns would swing almost close enough to hit."

A few minutes before 8:30 A.M., the *Mount Hood*'s supply officer left the ship in the captain's gig to visit the *Mindanao.*

At about the same time, another boat left the *Mount Hood* with a dozen men who were going ashore to get mail, return motion pictures, and go to sick call. They would be the *Mount Hood*'s only survivors.

The nearby *Mindanao* was a converted Liberty ship hull that carried about five hundred men, and a few minutes after 8:00 A.M., third-class metalsmith Bill Ryan would leave the quarterdeck after mustering for morning colors to go below to his duty station in the metal shop.

He was just getting to work when he was knocked off his feet by a tremendous force. He didn't hear the blast, but a big chunk of shrapnel tore a hole in the five-eighths-inch hull and flew past him, hitting a piece of machinery.

It was shortly after 8:30 A.M. that the *Mount Hood* was vaporized by an explosion that killed every man aboard. The blast, caused by an accidental detonation of ammunition, also killed or wounded 192 men on the *Mindanao*.

Another sailor on the beach later reported hearing a "thunderous, earsplitting roar (that) drowned out all other sounds in the harbor." The sailor saw the *Mount Hood* come out of the water, then fall back, to be covered by a cloud of smoke that mushroomed thousands of feet into the air. He saw all that before the shock wave hit him, flinging him back inside an aircraft hangar.

Another eyewitness was a mile and a half away, out in the harbor in a whaleboat, when the blast showered his small boat with debris, including one jagged piece of steel about the shape and size of a Christmas tree.

Back aboard the *Mindanao*, Bill Ryan picked himself up and ran for the hatches to go topside. The hatch covers were big timbers, which had been blown into the air, and when the timbers descended they came through the hatches like spears.

"Then we got hit by the shock wave," Bill recalled. "It was like a small tidal wave. The ship rolled way over on its side, and I got thrown down again. Everybody below decks wanted out. Men topside were yelling at us to stay below, but we finally made it to the top deck."

What greeted them was horror. Thirty-three holes, ranging in diameter from one foot to ten feet, had been punched in the side of the *Mindanao*. The ship's stack had a huge hole, torn when one of *Mount Hood*'s gun mounts passed through it. Everyone who'd been standing topside was either killed or injured, including the *Mount Hood*'s visiting supply officer.

"Maybe it was just scuttlebutt," Bill said. "But he came aboard our ship all the time because he didn't like all that ammunition handling on the *Mount Hood*."

Divers later discovered the explosion had cut a trench in the harbor floor that measured three hundred feet long by fifty feet wide and forty feet deep. When the human loss was finally tallied, this incident of "friendly fire" killed 386 sailors and wounded 372. Thirty-six large vessels and fifty-six smaller craft were damaged, but none so bad as the *Mindanao*.

Bill Ryan, age seventy-four, is the last of four survivors from Minnesota, and his memory of that day more than a half-century ago remains vivid.

"I was not injured, but when I got topside, I saw that the shock wave had rolled us over onto the tops of several small minesweepers that were tied up alongside. We literally pushed them under, and I saw sailors from the sweepers bobbing around like corks. Someone had a pet monkey, and he had crawled up a mast and was giving everybody holy hell.

"Then I saw a chief I knew on the main deck. He was wearing a really neat set of khakis, and it looked like he hadn't been scratched. I said something to him, and he replied, 'Excuse me, please,' and went over to the railing. I looked away for just a moment, looked back, and he was on the deck. Dead. There wasn't a mark on him, but the concussion killed him."

The survivors weren't given a lot of time to think about their good or bad luck, though. Repairs were under way almost immediately, and in just a few weeks the *Mindanao* returned to duty.

"There had been rumors that her keel was cracked, but we later went through a typhoon in Formosa (now Taiwan), and if that didn't break the ship, nothing else would. Ironically, the ship was later decommissioned and suffered her second and last explosion when it was mined and scuttled off Daytona Beach to form a fishing reef.

"I'll never forget that day in November 1944, though," said Bill. "What I remember the most vividly was sitting on the fantail after everything was over. A boat came around the back end of our ship, and it was the boat that had gone ashore from the *Mount Hood* earlier that morning. They were the *Hood*'s only survivors, and when they came around, they hollered, 'Where's our ship?' I couldn't say anything. I just couldn't say a thing. All I could do was point to where the water was still steaming and boiling.

"Nobody said anything, but they knew their ship was gone. And then they went away."

Margaret Was a Welder

OCTOBER 6, 1995

Early on in our visit, I learned how to address the lady. She is Margaret, not Maggie.

And she was a welder. She was not, I was informed, a bucker upper, a chin lifter, or even Rosie the Riveter.

That's how I met Margaret Kee, age eighty-four, of Grantsburg, Wisconsin, who demurely invited everyone to find a comfortable place to sit as she talked about the time her pants fell off in front of the soldiers.

Margaret belonged to the "hidden army" during World War II, the force of five million American women who went to work loading shells, operating cranes, painting ships, driving rivets, running lathes, and drilling holes in aircraft frames. That's what Margaret did at the Boeing plant in Seattle in 1942 for sixty-eight cents an hour.

More than fifty years later, Margaret's participation in the war effort was honored during Grantsburg High School's annual Patriots Day celebration.

To commemorate the end of the war, the high-school music department presented patriotic songs of the 1940s, when Rosie the Riveter at a defense plant in Milwaukee became the symbol of women throughout America who went to work wearing heavy gloves, slacks, and bandannas. Rosie's role in defense work was summed up in a 1943 Boeing publication this way:

"The woman on the business end of a rivet gun is closely akin to the soldier squeezing the trigger on his machine gun. Her rivets are bullets that she knows will be felt by the enemy. With every vibration of her rivet gun, she is giving the Axis a jolt."

Margaret, who lives in a Grantsburg senior center, is overjoyed but a bit mystified at the attention she is getting after all these years. In any event, she said, all she did was drill holes—"drill, not rivet, I drilled six holes for the riveters. Then, we had to grind the heads off the rivets they put in crooked."

Margaret first worked on B-19s, but "that plane was no good," so she spent most of her time building the fabled B-17 Flying Fortress.

"That was a good plane," she said. "We even signed the planes. We'd write 'Good luck' and sign our names to give the air crews a little lift."

Sometimes, the messages from the defense workers were saltier and more creative than that, said Dr. Jay P. Keepman, a Grantsburg physician who flew C-45 aircraft during the war. Keepman is Margaret's doctor, and he got her involved in the town celebration because he felt it was time she got some recognition for her labors. Whenever he razzes his patient about being Rosie the Riveter, she pointedly corrects him.

When war broke out in 1941, Margaret and her husband, Henry, a veteran of World War I, left Wisconsin for the West Coast because there were jobs there for men. When they got there, Henry went to work in a shipyard, and Margaret read that Boeing needed ten thousand women for its aircraft plant. Henry didn't want her to go to work, but she insisted; it was the Swiss and German in her, she says.

"I grabbed the chance to go to work as a mechanic. Women were making thirty-five or fifty cents an hour at canning factories, and at Boeing, we could make sixty-eight cents an hour. If I had stayed there a few more months, I would have made one dollar and sixteen cents per hour."

The men at the plant worked twelve-hour shifts, seven days a week. The women worked eight-hour shifts, she recalled.

"Rosie the Riveter," whose picture appeared on posters used all over America for recruitment, became the symbol of the women's work force. In the six months after Pearl Harbor, 750,000 women applied for defense jobs, but only eighty thousand were hired. It took awhile to change the attitude of many plant managers that women would pay too little attention to the machines and too much attention to the male workers.

"Many of the women got canned after working for a few months and paying their union dues," Margaret said. "The managers'd look for reasons, like saying their sweaters or slacks were too tight."

World War II was the first time women publicly wore slacks, and Margaret remembers the trouble they caused her when she was in Tacoma, Washington, once. Her slacks were being held up by a single safety pin, and just when a squad of soldiers marched by, that old pin gave out, and her slacks went south.

"I've not worn slacks since then," Margaret said.

Women who were called everything from "chin lifters" (they hoisted machine-gun turrets into position) to "bucker uppers" (riveters' helpers) eventually would account for a third of the aircraft-plant workers and ten percent of the employees at shipyards and in steel mills, where they did some of the toughest and dirtiest jobs.

And even though the government ruled that women should receive equal pay for equal work, their wages averaged only sixty percent of what the men made. Companies circumvented the regulation by reclassifying the jobs that women did.

As the war continued, married women and former housewives made up an increasingly large part of the work force. These were women who still had to go home, after their eight hours, to cook, clean, and care for children. The turnover among women employees was extraordinary (in four years, Boeing had to hire 250,000 women to maintain a work force of 39,000). Asked why more women did not go to work, one snapped, "Because they don't have wives."

Margaret and Henry Kee left Seattle, and their defense jobs, and went back to Wisconsin because the West Coast climate disagreed with Henry's asthma. Her role as Margaret the welder ended long before the war was over.

She has no photos from the era, she said; "My, no. We couldn't have cameras in those plants."

Henry died in 1970, and her two daughters are married and living elsewhere. Margaret has one memento of her time as a welder: a small red-white-and-blue metal ribbon with a capital E painted in red in the center, the E signifying "efficiency."

"That was hard work," she said, "standing up all the time, eight hours a day.

"No wonder my legs are shot."

Last Voyage of an LST

JANUARY 24, 2001

The audacious voyage of a World War II-era naval landing ship from the Isle of Crete in Greece to the United States began last November with an eloquent and memorable order from its skipper.

"Let's get the hell out of here right now," said Capt. Robert D. Jornlin. He had more than ample reason at the time to be fearful that he and his wizened, undermanned, and over-the-hill crew of seventy-five-year-old former sailors from World

War II and the Korean War might wind up in a Greek prison, a U.S. Coast Guard brig, or in some similar lockup as guests of the U.S. State Department.

That's how LST (Landing Ship Tank) 325 slipped away from Crete on the first leg of a fifty-two-day voyage that ended earlier this month with the ship steaming tenuously into Alabama's Mobile Bay on only one of its two tired engines.

The ship's electrician on this voyage was Gary C. Lyon, a salty old veteran of LST service during the Korean War. Gary, a retired civilian electrician from Local 110 of the International Brotherhood of Electrical Workers, and his wife, Gayle, live in Roseville.

"We were all volunteers, and everyone aboard had LST experience," said Gary after he'd gotten back to St. Paul last week. "But at first some of them thought this was the 'Love Boat,' and that we were going on a joy ride. Hardly!"

Now, an LST is not a sleek, elegant ship with the classic lines of a cruiser or a destroyer. Rather it looks like a 328-foot-long breadbox with massive doors that open out of its front end. It is called "landing ship tank" because it was designed to ferry twenty Sherman tanks and crews directly onto the beach, ready for battle.

Gary served on an LST that made several landings in Korea in the early 1950s and was also used to transport North Korean prisoners. He left the navy in 1956 as an electrician's mate, but he never got the saltwater completely wrung out of his socks.

He belongs to an organization of former LST sailors and was immediately interested when he first heard of a plan to find an operating LST somewhere in the world and bring it back to the United States for a museum.

"Some of the guys began discussing those possibilities ten years ago," said Gary, "and everybody said, 'Let's bring one home.' Beer was thought to have been involved."

As the plans got more and more serious, the LST group located vessels in Taiwan, Korea, Italy, Turkey, Greece, China, and Japan. Greece had three of them and was at first amenable to getting rid of one because that would enable the Greek navy to get a newer surplus ship from the United States.

Through recruiting and volunteering, seventy-four tough old sailors were soon on the crew roster. Each man put up two thousand dollars for expenses, and each of them passed a physical to ensure they were fit for the trip. Even if everyone on that original roster had made the voyage, the crew would have been far short of the normal complement of 108. It meant that each man worked at least twelve hours a day, seven days a week, throughout the voyage.

The prevoyage problems began developing almost immediately. The first contingent that went to Greece managed to get the Greeks angry, and Gary said it soon became clear that the Clinton administration, including the State Department and the Coast Guard, was not in support of the trip.

"One admiral said in an interview we'd never make it because the ship was too old and the crew was too old, too few, and too inexperienced. He said the whole thing was unsafe. He made us so mad we all told him to go to hell."

Gary had to assemble a uniform of sorts out of work clothes he found at Fleet Farm, and by October, he was finally on his way to Greece. It would be his job to keep all the electric motors in the ship working.

The ship had been used as a transport vessel by the Greeks, but it was filthy, and its engines had not worked for three years. Finally, by November 5, the ship was ready to sail, but there were still some minor impediments, such as a lack of insurance, an absence of life rafts, an American embassy that would not allow the LST to fly the U.S. flag, and one Greek admiral who threatened to put the whole crew in jail if they tried to leave.

The crew was also down to thirty-two men by then. The ship desperately needed fuel to get under way (it got some from a British petroleum source), and still it somehow escaped from Souda Bay, Crete, on November 14.

"It took us thirteen days to get to Gibraltar," said Gary, "and nine of the days were stormy, with up to fifty-mile-an-hour headwinds and twelve- to sixteen-foot swells running. An LST acts very poorly in rough water. It tends to twist and bend."

And things broke down. After the LST finally got under way from Gibraltar to the United States on December 12, the steering system broke and had to be jerry-rigged with a set of handles that worked like a Nintendo game. The automatic washing machine regularly broke down and caught on fire, and it was Gary's job to fix it, which he did by manufacturing a new manual system using light bulbs to advise the operator when to change cycles.

"We lost another engine in December, and instead of steaming at nine miles per hour, we were making about three or four miles per hour. The poor old girl was just banging and clattering. Whenever we'd start the engine, it would belch black smoke and there'd be this terrible sound like that pink submarine in the movie *Operation Petticoat.*"

Once, when the throttle wouldn't stay in its proper position, Gary fixed it using an empty Tylenol bottle as a buffer.

On top of breakdowns, the voyage to Mobile was accompanied by bad weather. Of fifty-two days at sea, forty were stormy.

They also lost several members of the crew who left the ship in Gibraltar. For the last, longest leg of the 4,350-mile cruise, they were down to twenty-eight men and a photographer.

And then there was the chow.

"The cook was a baker from Alaska, and cooking was not his forte," said Gary, who lost thirty pounds on the voyage. "The cook just couldn't keep up, and he got tired. By the end of the trip, the freezers were full of good meat, but we were eating Spam, lots of Spam, and peanut butter-and-jelly sandwiches."

But they steamed, somewhat lamely, into Mobile Bay on January 10.

More than one hundred other ships escorted them to their

final destination, and the tired crew was reunited with their families. The ship that shouldn't have sailed in the first place was brought home by a crew of old sailors whose ages ranged from sixty-eight (Gary was the youngest) to seventy-seven.

Would he do it again?

"No. None of us would. We worked too long, too hard, in heat that got up to one hundred and seventeen degrees. It was like living in an oven.

"No, I would not do it again. But I'm sure glad we made it home without help from anyone."

Chosin Reservoir and Heartbreak Ridge

SEPTEMBER 6, 1998

Being a Minnesota boy, Arnold Del Castillo knew cold weather, but the winter of 1950 went straight to his soul. His socks were frozen tight to his feet for many days, and if frosted toes weren't bad enough, 120,000 Chinese Communist soldiers were trying to kill him.

"I can still hear their bugles and their whistles and their hollering when they came at us at night," said Del Castillo, one of the U.S. Marine Corps "Chosin Few" who survived the historic withdrawal from the Chosin Reservoir in the fiercest fighting of the Korean War.

"To this day," Del Castillo said quietly, "I do not know how I made it."

The ordeal of the 1st Marine Division at Chosin Reservoir in North Korea almost fifty years ago is seared into the memory of the tough old Leatherneck. Now, on the eve of the dedication of a State Capitol Mall monument to their service in Korea, Del Castillo and other veterans of the "Forgotten War" remember the conflict from which they somehow came home.

Del Castillo is sixty-eight, a survivor of both Korea and

aortic heart surgery. Augie Garcia of Roseville was sixty-seven when he died, and Ed Schurmeier of Woodbury is sixty-nine. Their terrible old war has been forgotten by some, but not by them, nor by any of the seventy-nine thousand Minnesota men and thirteen hundred women who served during the Korean War era and for whom the dramatic monument just south of the Capitol was constructed.

America's involvement in a fighting war in Korea lasted for only about three years, from 1950 to an ambiguous armistice in 1953, but almost fifty-five thousand Americans died there, about the same number that were lost in ten years in Vietnam. Del Castillo faced death at the Chosin Reservoir during the thirty-below-zero winter of 1950, and war came later to Garcia and Schurmeier at bloody places called Heartbreak Ridge, the Punch Bowl, the Golden Nugget, and the Iron Triangle.

Del Castillo was already a veteran of almost four years in the marines and had only six months left to serve when his enlistment was extended in 1950. His older brothers had served in World War II, and all of a sudden he found himself in a new war when the marines landed at the port city of Inchon in history's last massive amphibious assault.

"September 15, 1950," Del Castillo said, as though the date were a long-remembered birthday or a family anniversary. "We took Inchon and then Seoul and moved north, fighting our way up to this Chosin Reservoir."

Corporal Del Castillo's job was to protect the ammunition and make sure it found its way to his battalion's riflemen and anti-tank gunners. He vividly recalls the convoys moving northward through narrow mountain passes and the feeling that someone was watching them. He'd heard about how good the North Koreans were at camouflaging themselves.

The landing at Inchon had gone so well that the generals decided to keep heading north across the Thirty-Eighth Parallel to unite the divided country under one flag. One army division even made it across the Yalu River into Manchuria.

What the Americans didn't know was that three hundred

thousand Chinese Communist troops were ready to strike from the north and push the army division in a 275-mile retreat. And the Chinese army's X Corps also sprang the trap at the Chosin Reservoir, determined to wipe out an entire U.S. Marine division—Del Castillo's.

"There were one hundred and twenty thousand of them and twelve thousand marines," Del Castillo said. "We fought day and night for more than a week. On top of the fighting, you wouldn't believe how cold it got, thirty to thirty-five below zero with the wind blowing. My Korean boots were too hot on my feet, and when I took my regular boots off, my socks were frozen to my feet.

"We would not leave our dead behind, and one time I had to go up a ravine after two bodies. We were taking fire from both sides. Nine days at that reservoir . . . it seemed like an eternity. They were throwing everything they had at us, and at night they would come within ten yards of us in those bugle attacks. We just piled them up . . . "

Del Castillo heard that many marines were executed after they ran out of ammunition. That was not going to happen to him, so he armed himself well with a rifle, a carbine, a submachine gun, and a German Luger he'd liberated from a dead enemy soldier in Seoul.

"I would say I was always afraid, but I was never scared. There's a difference, and I only survived because of my training. I lost a lot of friends over there, and I learned something about myself. I learned how to survive and that I can handle just about anything that comes along."

Del Castillo's 1st Marine Division was finally ordered to retreat, to "advance in a different direction," and the marines then fought their way seventy-six miles south to Hungnam, where a gigantic sea-lift evacuated U.S. and South Korean troops, civilians, and supplies.

Time magazine later called the ordeal at Chosin Reservoir "America's worst military licking since Pearl Harbor" and "the worst defeat America has ever suffered." Del Castillo's division had 2,103 casualties—343 dead, 78 missing, and 1,683 wounded.

"And all I got," said Del Castillo, who came back to construction work after the Korean War and who has two daughters, eight grandchildren, and four great-grandchildren, "was cold."

War for Augie Garcia of the West Side came a bit later. He was digging ditches for Northern States Power when he was drafted into the army early in 1952 at the age of nineteen. After basic training, he went straight to Korea and an artillery battalion. Like Del Castillo, he landed at Inchon, except that by 1952 American forces had battled back from the Chosin Reservoir retreat, and both sides had settled in for a seesaw siege along a no-man's land near the Thirty-Eighth Parallel.

"We got on trucks at Inchon, and after a few hours we were at the front lines," Garcia later recalled. "It was pitch dark, but I could hear small-arms fire, and the sky looked like a lightning storm. All of a sudden, a door to a bunker opened, light shone out for a moment, and I was inside. I was a replacement, and that meant some guy was going home. All I heard was, 'He's mine, he's mine.'"

"One guy was on a phone and someone said, 'Fire mission!' and everyone was out of there in fifteen seconds. I followed them, and there I was, loading and firing a 155 mm. howitzer. Welcome to the war—it scared the (bleep) out of me, though. I didn't know what to expect, and the next morning we moved the guns. We were constantly moving the guns so they would be harder to hit."

Garcia's position was in rolling hills overlooking Heartbreak Ridge, where some of the toughest fighting of the war took place.

"We supported the infantry attacks, usually at night, when most of the fighting went on. By day, we could see the enemy playing volleyball. Then, during an attack, we'd take incoming artillery fire and listen for the whine of the shells going over and a crack, like lightning, when they'd hit somewhere."

One day, Garcia didn't hear the whine because it didn't go all the way over. He heard the crack, and it was the bunker he was in, taking a direct hit.

"I was buried under logs, dirt, and rock, and it took the other troops about an hour and a half to dig us out. My back and neck hurt so badly that I felt like I'd been dragged around behind a car."

For his wounds, Garcia later got the Purple Heart. At the time, though, he was back on duty the following day. In recent years, he has had throat cancer. He thought there may be some connection between his wounds and the cancer, but his records were destroyed in a fire, and even though he had photos of his bombed-out bunker, he did not have enough proof of his injury to qualify for any kind of medical assistance.

"I stayed on the line through two winters," he said, "and I remember pulling out under attack one time, following a big truck full of Korean wounded. You could see the blood pouring out through the tailgate."

Augie Garcia finally did get out of combat and he did come home, where two weeks later he was back in the ditches for NSP. If you were around in the middle and late 1950s, you probably remember Augie Garcia's music. He and his band brought rock 'n' roll to Minnesota, with songs like "Hi Yo Silver" and "Drinking Wine, Spo-Dee O-Dee," but in the years just before his death, the cancer would put an end to his singing career.

Ed Schurmeier's life now gives no clue as to what he went through as a young man. After a career in the computer industry—and the restaurant business in which he's owned and operated popular spots in Minnesota and Wisconsin— he's a maitre d' at trendy Sunsets Restaurant in Woodbury.

Soft-spoken, white-haired, and unfailingly polite, Schurmeier once carried a Browning automatic rifle into infantry operations in deadly places with names like the Punch Bowl, the Golden Nugget, and, of course, Heartbreak Ridge.

It was 1951, and like Del Castillo before him and Garcia after him, Schurmeier's war began with a landing at Inchon.

"It was eighty percent boredom and twenty percent pure terror," he recalled. "Everything that can happen to you is pretty stupid, so you avoid trees that can set off airburst shells that spray downward, you don't make yourself a silhouette on a ridge line, you walk where others have walked because of mines, and you use your head. And I still got blown off a ridge one time."

And burned when a mortar blew up a tent he was in. Schurmeier spent three weeks in a MASH unit and was told the burns on his foot would never heal unless he was sent home.

"Then the b——d started to heal. They gave me an oversize boot and three pairs of socks and sent me back up to the line.

"It was like a big king of the hill game. You work hard to gain some ground, then you give it up. It didn't make any sense to work that hard and then give it up.

"But I was just a grunt, just trying to survive. This is the most I've ever talked about it, and I can tell you this: Unless you were there, you can't fully understand it.

"And," Schurmeier added wryly, "I would have gotten along just fine in life without that war."

Memorial Hall and One of Its Sons

OCTOBER 17, 1990

Donald Bradehoft wrote to Leo and Lil Carle from Camp Polk in Louisiana, where he had become "a regular old tank driver."

"I can make one of these babies stand on its hind feet now. At one time, I always wanted to drive a tank, (and) I sure will miss them when I have to leave them."

But most of all, Donald wanted to be at home with his

wife, Rosie, and their child, Martin, "and I'll be the happiest guy in the world."

Meanwhile, he wrote, "Tell Leo I'd like to get him in a tank alongside of me in the assistant driver's seat. I sure would give him a ride. Ask him how he'd like to take a ride with me. I guess I've fired darn near every kind of gun the Army has got—the fifty-caliber machine gun, the thirty-caliber machine gun, the Thompson submachine gun, the Garand rifle, and the forty-five-caliber automatic. I didn't think I'd make such a good soldier, but I guess I was lucky. I'm assigned to my own tank and am a regular driver."

Donald then went on to tell Leo and Lil at length about his love for Rosie and the child. The pages of his letter are yellowed and fragile, and the penciled writing is dim and smudged in places. Love to all, the soldier wrote, and then he closed. It was January 30, 1943.

Donald Bradehoft was always a very special nephew of the Carles, having lived with them on and off from the time he was fifteen until he got married and then went away in 1942. Lil remembered the day he came home in his new uniform to say good-bye and how Queenie, their collie-shepherd with the sweet face, crawled up under the heavy brown army greatcoat he was carrying.

"See?" said Donald. "Even Queenie knows." Then he went away to the war.

Designers of the St. Paul City Hall and Ramsey County Courthouse meant for its eighty-five-foot-long Memorial Hall to be a great shrine to the fallen veterans of the county. The engraved, gilded names of the World War I dead that look upon the God of Peace statue came with the building when it was dedicated in 1931. Later wars added to the toll: 952 members of the armed services from Ramsey County died in World War II; 70 were killed in Korea; 150 in Vietnam. Their names were meant to be carved in the walls, but a succession of politicians always found other ways to spend the money.

The names are there now, the World War II dead on the

lower two floors and those from Korea and Vietnam on the third floor. The money for the twenty-five thousand dollar sandblasting project came from twenty-seven Ramsey County VFW posts, and the hall was rededicated this year on Veterans Day.

The boys at city hall let us in last Sunday morning. Leo and Lil and their daughter, Kathy, and I walked through the dim, silent, Memorial Hall to the low, tunnel-like corridor that flanks the west side of the hall's first floor. The blue, almost black, marble walls are freshly carved at eye level, and soft, indirect light tumbles down on the names from above.

When we found it, we all silently moved our fingers across the name of Sgt. Donald R. Bradehoft, a twenty-three-year-old tank driver who died in Holland in 1944. I did not know my wife's cousin, but his family never felt closer to him.

In the Trenches for Korean Vets

JULY 21, 1997

Sally has traded her billboard for a bunker, and she's back in business. The remembering business.

Sally Adams is Bunker Sally now, currently bivouacked by her sandbag bungalow in the parking lot of a South St. Paul saloon. She'll be wherever the bunker is, come heat, high winds, rain, hail, sleet, or pestilence until enough money is raised to build the Minnesota Korean War Veterans Memorial on the Capitol Mall in St. Paul.

Sally, sixty-four, of Delano, is a veteran at this lonely duty. In the autumn of 1991, she voluntarily occupied a pup tent twenty-five feet above the ground on the ledge of a freeway billboard outside Forest Lake.

Sally maintained her tenuous perch to raise public consciousness, and money, to complete the Minnesota Vietnam

Veterans Memorial. Somewhere along the line she was dubbed "Billboard Sally," and after three weeks of high living on the billboard she reached her goal of raising seventy-three thousand dollars—fifty thousand of that in one chunk from a Golden Valley businessman.

The businessman, Bill Popp, said he was impressed with her commitment to the cause of the veterans and her willingness to stay at her precarious outpost. The Vietnam vets memorial became a reality and was completed and dedicated in September 1992.

This time, the goal is to remember the Minnesota veterans who served during the Korean War. This was the "forgotten war," the war in which 700 Minnesotans were killed, 1,500 were wounded, and 154 are still listed as missing in action.

By 1996, the Minnesota legislature had appropriated a total of three hundred thousand dollars for the memorial and then left it to the Korean War Veterans Memorial Association to raise the other three hundred thousand dollars needed to build the monument. Sally and the vets did raise their share; the memorial was built and dedicated on September 13, 1998.

Sally said she wants her fourteen grandchildren to be able to go to that memorial and be reminded of the debt that is owed America's war veterans.

She's traced her family back to the French and Indian War, and subsequent ancestors fought in the Revolutionary War, the Civil War, and World Wars I and II.

Her first husband, Donald Smith, who died in 1971, was a navy veteran of the Korean War, and her present husband, Larry Adams, is an air force vet. Sally's son, Dennis Michael Smith, is a combat veteran of Vietnam.

"When the call came," she said, "our family went."

A Knack for
Knowing Things

The Guardian Angel of Lower St. Clair

APRIL 14, 1999

Carl Bentson knows things, so many, many things. He knows precisely when the automobile plant in Kenosha, Wisconsin, folded; he knows when the A pod, the B pod, and the C pod of his school in St. Paul were recarpeted; he knows how many miles it is to Tim's place at Schroeder, Minnesota; and he knows which Cadillac he likes the best. That would be the '59 with the big tail fins.

Some would say Carl Bentson has disabilities, and young men have egged him and his house because he is different and stands out when he pedals around the West End on his big old tricycle, the one with all the lights, the homemade top, and the reflectors.

If there are disabilities, though, they'd be primarily in the minds of those who would put limits on Carl. He has ridden that trike to Red Wing, Forest Lake, Lindstrom, and Taylors Falls. He pedals it to car shows at RiverCentre and the Minnesota State Fairgrounds and to the Mall of America to build things in Lego Land. He pulls a coaster wagon with his trike at his neighborhood block parties so he can give the little children rides, and he runs errands for his neighbors. Carl has got fifty-six thousand miles on that chariot.

Carl is thirty-six and works at the Bridgeview special-needs school, from which he graduated almost fifteen years ago. He owns a home on the West End, and he barbecues, bakes, shovels, weeds, and cuts grass for all his neighbors. In his spare time, he mends library books and defies stereotypes about people who are born to be special.

"Carl is the guardian angel of lower St. Clair Avenue," said Dr. Tim Rumsey, a West End physician, author, and good friend to Carl. "He is a savant, someone whose verbal skills would test out in a very low range but whose performance I.Q.

is in the genius range. Carl is very much like the 'Rain Man' when it comes to cars. He knows everything about the automobile."

That comes from reading everything he can, at his own gradual pace, about the automobile. It comes, said Bill Burrington, his supervisor at Bridgeview School, from memorizing window stickers at all the car dealerships on University Avenue. It comes from pedaling his trike out to Porky's Drive-in on University on Friday and Saturday nights for the classic-car street shows.

By day, Carl is part of the custodial staff at Bridgeview and is described by Burrington as an "exceptional employee." Carl's forte is washing, mopping, and picking up. He is such an enthusiastic picker-up of refuse and trash that he often goes off the school grounds after it and must be reminded that there is no requirement that he clean up the railroad tracks or the nearby private yards.

He is just as fastidious on his own block of St. Clair Avenue, his neighbors say. His neat little house is always decorated to honor the major holidays. The Easter bunnies were just up, and soon there will be something for Memorial Day and then the Fourth of July. By then, Carl will be well into his ambitious summer lawn maintenance program, for his yard and for those of his neighbors.

"He is a community asset," said a neighbor, Mary Ziemer. "The neighbors watch out for him, and he watches out for us. He's a character we all love and are lucky to have around us."

When Carl was egged by a group of young men, Mary helped him write a poster asking for any information on the incident. Carl passed out copies of the poster all the way from West Seventh Street to Crocus Hill.

"Three kids," Carl said. "They got out of a Prizm and threw eggs on me. That's like that guy who threw pie at the governor. It's mean, and they shouldn't do it."

Carl was born in Winnebago, Minnesota, and given up by his parents. He spent his early years at Cambridge State Hospital, where he stayed until the hospital was closed in the early 1960s. After that, he was fortunate to be one of the 162 foster children of Vashti Risdall, one of Ramsey County's premier foster mothers.

"Twenty-three years," Carl said. "May 10, 1967, to October 12, 1990."

From the age of four, Carl has been part of Vashti Risdall's family, and he still pedals to her house in the Macalester-Groveland neighborhood once or twice a week "to see Grandma. She's ninety-six, but she's up and about."

He has owned his own home since 1990, and Carl cherishes his independence and ability to cook.

"I cook everything and barbecue out front while I watch the traffic go by. Last night I cooked lamb chops. I do fish, chicken, hamburger, and hot dishes. Once in a while, I'll bake a cake."

Does he feel in any way handicapped?

"Not with all the things I can do. I travel all over. Tim Rumsey and I went up to Lake Superior and cleaned out his cabin. Eighty miles north of Duluth. You know the name of that place? It's on the milk cartons."

Carl enjoyed his riddle and waited for an answer. When it didn't come, he grinned and said, "Schroeder. That's where Tim's cabin is."

"The trip was absolutely wonderful because Carl is a joy to be with," said Rumsey. "As we went by towns along the freeway, he was calling off all the populations because he'd read all about them before we went. His memory for detail is absolutely astounding. Especially when it comes to cars."

Carl is always ready to talk about cars. It doesn't bother him not to drive them, he said, as long as he can look at them, read about them, and draw pictures of them accurate to the smallest detail.

"The new ones have better technology," Carl said. "They have front-wheel drive and four-wheel drive. That's good. And they used to make Renaults in Kenosha and then they folded."

But he also likes the classics, which he sees on weekends when he pedals out to Porky's for the University Avenue street show.

"The fifty-nine Cadillac with the big fins. That's my favorite. They had 390s in them and all kinds of buttons. They started out at five thousand dollars, base price. With all the buttons, eight thousand dollars. Today, that would be forty-two thousand dollars."

Carl's memory for all sorts of information is helpful to his employers, Bill Burrington said. When the school wanted to redecorate, no one could remember how old the carpeting was. No one but Carl, who matter-of-factly reported the years that each section of the school was done.

"And the cafeteria," Carl added.

"He remembers when members of the staff come and when they go," Burrington said. "He shows up for all the school functions, and for weddings, no matter where they are, and graduation parties . . . "

"They are all my friends," Carl said.

Carl Bentson is just as highly regarded in his neighborhood.

"He loves to garden but absolutely hates dandelions," said his neighbor and friend Karen Koeppe. "He hates them with a passion. Heaven help anyone in the neighborhood who might like to make dandelion wine because there aren't any around. Carl pulls them all.

"And he's interested in everything," she added. "He goes to Confederate Air Shows, street rod rallies, car shows. We walked into one of those, and he knew so much about the cars by heart that those salesmen in their $350 suits stood and listened to him with their mouths hanging open.

"And he draws the cars to perfection. And he likes to pedal to the airport and watch the planes land. He likes hardware stores and Home Depot, he likes to dress up and go to dinner, and he asks 'Why?' all the time. He wants to know why."

Karen stops to think about her friend.

"We are so proud of Carl, with what he's done with his life. He wants to live to be one hundred."

"I have a good life," Carl said.

He Could Do Anything

MAY 23, 1998

There arose a terrible racket from the upper reaches of the church. The words of the preacher were all but drowned out Easter Sunday by this unholy metallic cacophony, and everyone wondered when someone was going to do something.

Ted Anderson, naturally, went quietly to the back of the church, up into the balcony, and then up some more, in his best Sunday suit, into the dark and musty reaches of the belfry and beyond. He climbed to the absolute summit of the sanctuary, restored quiet to a clangorous fan motor, and then returned to his seat in the church without a word. Ted had done it again.

In this little church community, it was Ted who could do anything, again and again. Ted was there before sunup to plow the snow, and in years gone by, he'd go out with one of his homemade flatbed trailers and round up the loftiest Christmas tree that could be stuffed through the doors of First Lutheran Church in St. Paul. Twenty or thirty feet of tree would be hauled in somehow, raised upright with gadgets fabricated by Ted and then installed—nailed, bolted, and turnbuckled into the church floor—by Ted.

I never knew a man who could do more with a logging chain, a block-and-tackle, come-along winches, and some wretched and worn-out vehicle that had been rescued from demolition like a mongrel from the dog pound. If Ted didn't have the right truck to haul a huge Christmas tree, a dozen boat docks to the lake, or a stock car to the race track, he'd make one.

I'm not sure when I met Ted, but it was more than thirty years ago. He picked me up before sunup one Saturday morning in either an old school bus or a deservedly retired water department dump truck, and we headed for the camp our church operates on an island in northern Minnesota.

What tools should I bring, I'd earlier asked Ted.

"You won't need to bring tools," he said.

What will we be doing, I asked. He thought about the question for a long moment, as he usually did, and then said all I had to do was to move a cabin. Where would you like it moved, I asked.

"Up into the air," Ted said, grinning, "but no more than three or four feet."

And we moved that cabin up into the air, with Ted's massive house jacks and his shrewd engineering, high enough to put four courses of blocks and a dry, new floor under it.

A few years later, I wound up somehow as chairman of the camp committee, and Ted officially had to let me in on the planning for his never-ending camp improvement program.

"I think we need some new docks," Ted said, so we went out one day and looked at all kinds of expensive commercial docks that came ingeniously built on wheels so they could be rolled right into and out of the water. We finally found some that seemed sturdy enough to meet Ted's very high standards for durability.

The next time I talked to Ted about purchasing the docks, he said, "I built a few." He'd built about eight of them, out of heavy steel he had liberated from scrapyards. The rolling docks he had made were sturdy enough to land aircraft on. All he had needed from the dock store was a design he could improve on.

Ted worked forty-two years in a foundry in St. Paul, ran things, I've heard, and that would not be surprising. While others stand around talking about what must be done, Ted would have already moved into action. Hands of steel and raw mechanical genius were tempered in Ted with subtle wit and a gentle thoughtfulness that made him a special Sunday school teacher, quite literally for generations.

Ted Anderson would be the perfect lifeboat companion, I decided long ago. When all about you is going desperately bad, you probably don't need the politician, the policeman, the lawyer, the urban planner, the college professor, or the newspaper reporter. You need Ted to get the electricity working, the motor running, and everything and everyone headed in the right direction.

Ted Anderson was around that camp on Bay Lake near Aitken his whole life, and his signature is in sturdy works all over the place: at a famous and popular outdoor chapel set on the wooded shore, in cabins built and rebuilt, and in the network of Ted's aircraft-carrier docks. This is where Ted was working last Saturday, the last day of his life.

Ted Anderson, sixty-two, was killed on the island at Bay Lake when something went horribly wrong during a tree removal project, and he was crushed by a truck.

A huge crowd of friends and congregation members gathered at our church Thursday morning for Ted's funeral, and later that day, he was buried in Union Cemetery in Maplewood, alongside his wife, Janet, who died in 1992.

The sudden, tragic loss last week left the people of Ted's little community wondering how they can get along without him, wondering who will plow the snow, who will climb to the top of the church to make the noise go away. And wondering who will take care of Ted Anderson's cherished Bay Lake Camp.

Baking Bread by the Carload

JUNE 23, 2001

There is an inclination to approach a ninety-five-year-old nun with a certain amount of caution, as though what you are dealing with is a fragile and ancient artifact. I was not prepared for Sister Mary Regina McCabe.

In our first few minutes together in the parlors of the Convent of Visitation School in Mendota Heights, she talked of making bread by the carload, of how deeply she loathes capital punishment, and how much she enjoys riding horses, following the Twins and the Vikings, and being marooned in the middle of a buffalo herd.

It is no wonder that she is the darling of Visitation Convent, this miniature Sissy Spacek with the deep alto voice of Lauren Bacall. A couple of weeks ago, the Visitation community celebrated Sister Mary Regina's seventy-fifth anniversary as a nun, and when she learned it was to be a catered affair, she said the only way she'd take part is if she could make the bread herself, which she did.

In fact, she makes twenty-five loaves several times each week, with the help of her Hobart electric mixer, as well as ice cream for the seventeen sisters in the Visitation community. On baking days, she starts the bread at 6:00 A.M., letting it rise until 9:00 or 10:00 A.M., when she puts it in to bake.

And if she is at some crucial point in the baking process when community prayer begins, she has a "dispensation" and doesn't have to go. One of the perks of seniority.

"We call her our scullery knave around here," said Sister Marie Therese Conaty, mother superior at Visitation.

"Well, yes," said Sister Mary Regina, "peeling parsnips, making ice cream, baking all the bread and the prayers five times a day—that all keeps me pretty busy."

The life of Sister Mary Regina is captured in a seventy-six-page, first-person narrative, "What the Lord Wanted," just produced by Catherine Condon Sicard, a former Visitation student.

"I had this machine in front of me, and I just talked into it," said Sister Mary Regina. "I had no idea it was going to be so long."

Not long enough, though. The little book is a delightful collection of how a child born in Staples, Minnesota, in 1906 was christened Eleanor Claire McCabe and grew up in Belfield, North Dakota, on the edge of the Badlands.

Her father was a businessman out there, and it is plain from her words that she adored him. He had the first car in Belfield but was a "horrible" driver.

"One didn't need a driver's license then, especially in North Dakota, where there was nothing to hit."

She was the fifth of eight children, and like her sisters, she would eventually be sent back to St. Paul to attend the original Visitation Convent at Fairmount Avenue and Grotto Street.

And when it came time for Eleanor to attend college, she lasted exactly one semester at the College of St. Catherine. She said she felt disconnected, homesick, and unhappy.

"One day, I decided I wasn't going back. I just walked out." She'd made up her mind to become a nun and returned to Visitation. "This is what I will do," she decided, and the cloistered, contemplative life of a Visitation sister is what she wanted and what she knows her Lord wanted for her.

She took her final vows seventy-five years ago and, unlike most of her colleagues, never gave up the traditional black habit, even though the rules of dress were greatly modified through the years.

The book is full of candid photos of Sister Mary Regina and her family. She never got over her love of riding horses, and one photo from 1997 shows her next to a horse and wearing a big cowboy hat over her habit. Another shows her on a stepladder wearing a hard hat over her habit.

She also talks about the time not long ago that she was riding through the hills of North Dakota with a nephew when their vehicle was suddenly surrounded by a herd of 150 wild buffalo. The animals began banging and bumping the car around.

"It was scary. They're very stupid. At the same time, they're mean. One must never cross them." She asked her nephew how they were going to get out of this fix.

"You just wait," he said. "Quietly."

"And we did."

Sister Mary Regina taught for many years and was elected mother superior of her community, serving from 1963 to 1969, the period when the monastery and school moved from St. Paul to a much larger, suburban setting in Mendota Heights.

One might expect a sister of such stature to be somewhat reserved and even austere, but Sister Mary Regina is refreshingly candid with her ideas and opinions.

She worked in Visitation's drama department once but hated it because, "Mostly what I did was drag out the costumes, sit through eternal rehearsals, and clean up after the shows."

In later years, she happily traded teaching for baking bread, and now she stays busy, "baking bread, listening to ragtime music on the radio, watching the Minnesota Vikings and the Twins, and reading."

"I love to read, but I hate capital punishment," she said, reflecting on all the recent stories about the execution of Oklahoma City bomber Timothy McVeigh.

"I never prayed so hard in my life as I did for that McVeigh. I just do not believe in capital punishment. We have no right to take the life of anyone."

She'd also like to register some choice opinions about the current leadership of the country, but her younger colleagues, Sister Perrone Marie Thibert, a former mother superior, and Sister Marie Therese warmly cautioned her that we were all there to talk about baking bread and celebrating anniversaries.

"Well, I'm full of hope for the future," Sister Mary Regina said with a great smile. "I'm going to God soon!"

Ascending the Shoreview TV Tower

OCTOBER 18, 1993

Bill Farrell proved what kind of guy he is the first time he went to the top of Channel Nine's Shoreview TV tower.

"The engineer who'd been up there a hundred times, maybe two hundred times, had hold of the tower with both hands. I, however, was holding on with just one hand."

That's because Farrell's other hand was occupied. It had a firm grip on his rosary.

Somehow Farrell and his rosary found themselves going again to the top of the tower one day recently, along with Channel Nine engineering technician Dick Sigurdson and a newspaper columnist who's never learned how simply to say, "No thanks."

Some nomenclature: the three TV antennas in Shoreview are the tallest things around. Nothing else comes anywhere close, unless you'd stack two IDS towers one on top of another. From the top of Channel Nine's tower, you're looking straight down at almost 1,466 feet of pure Shoreview air, and from the top, I'd guess on a clear day you could see just about as far as you'd want to see if you'd open your eyes. Golly, that's a long way up—and an electrifying ride to boot.

"Keep your hands inside the metal door," said Dick, as the three of us squeezed together inside an elevator (none of this climbing business) half the size of Superman's phone booth.

"In fact, don't even touch anything metal when we go on by these FM stations on the tower. There's a lot of radio-frequency energy bouncing around up here. I guess you could get yourself microwaved. Can you feel it tingle yet? I hear it hits your eyes the worst. And your gonads."

Wheeee.

Farrell's ascension of the tower was actually a homecoming

of sorts. He was mayor of Shoreview in September 1971 when a newly installed companion transmission tower used by TV, WCCO, and WTCN (forerunner to KARE) collapsed one morning, killing seven men, some of whom were in the tower and others on the ground. An investigation by the Minnesota Department of Labor and Industry later put the blame for the collapse on faulty welding. Witnesses said one leg of the tower suddenly buckled, bringing the five-hundred-ton structure down in a heap.

Channel Nine's tower just to the east also had just been completed, and following the accident, Farrell said, there was speculation that it, too, might be on the verge of catastrophe.

"I decided the mayor would have to go to the top to demonstrate how safe it was," said Farrell. "I remember so vividly looking down on the collapsed tower nearby. It looked like a bowl of steel spaghetti."

The ruined tower has since been replaced by two 1,375-foot towers, and Channel Nine's antenna is now a fully laden Christmas tree of FM stations and TV transmitters. In addition to Channel Nine, the signals from channels Two, Seventeen, Twenty-three, and Twenty-nine go off the tower, as do the broadcasts from KQRS, KRXX, KTCZ, KTIS, KSJN, KDWB, KEEY, WLTE, and, most recently, WBOB.

"For good or ill," said Farrell, "Shoreview is known as the home of the TV towers. Even the pine trees on Shoreview's official logo are often mistaken for TV towers. When people hear that you're from Shoreview, they always say, 'Isn't that where that tower fell down years ago?'"

The tower is a triangular arrangement of three nine-inch posts held together with cross members and steadied by three sets of seven guy wires anchored in huge concrete pads several hundred yards from the tower. The tower does not sway in heavy wind; rather, it "torques," said Sigurdson, who gets to go up regularly to change the tower's array of light bulbs.

There is a steel ladder one could climb all the way to the top—pranksters have scaled aloft to fly their school colors, said Sigurdson—but the most sensible way is by elevator, a trip that takes about fifteen minutes each way.

All around the tower at the top of the elevator ride are challenging graffiti left by the iron workers who built the structure.

"What are you looking at?" one message asks. In the case of the columnist, nothing except the most convenient hand-hold. There is a small rectangular platform at the top, about the size of a door mat, and it's just steel mesh you can see through to give that added sense of vulnerability.

The elevator does not actually go all the way to the top of the tower. Channel Nine's transmitting mast goes up another seventy to ninety feet, accessible only by ladder.

That was a trip that neither Farrell nor any of his companions that day was interested in making. Think about that climb for a moment. It's enough to make you tingle without any radio frequency energy bouncing around.

Making Music in the Park

AUGUST 16, 1993

The conductor in the familiar red dinner jacket fought his way upwind to a handhold at the microphone. His face was a pinkish beam upon his audience, his green eyes down to narrow slits behind horn-rimmed glasses, and his teeth were clenched in a cheerful grimace that made him look as though he were racing the breeze aboard a big Harley. The entertainment would start, he announced in his sweet, gentle rasp, "just as soon as we get the music glued down."

A stiff south wind ripped across the stage of the promenade at the Como Lake Pavilion and tore at the musicians' sheet music. Volunteers were summoned from the audience and stationed among the music stands to keep the pages from flying away, and even at that, every now and then a page full of the "William Tell" Overture took off for the golf course.

But the Sunday afternoon park pops concert plunged on, and on, as the director in the familiar red dinner jacket clutched his music with one hand and with the other led his nineteen musicians and intrepid soloists through the "Washington Post March," "Hello Dolly," and a couple of Strauss waltzes. Max Metzger is the faithful old letter carrier of the musical world; neither rain, nor sleet, nor gloom of night, nor swooping geese, nor noisy skaters, nor barking dogs, nor outbound aircraft, nor tornado warnings shall stay Max from the eventual delivery of his appointed concert.

Nothing on earth could stop Max from producing music at Como, and he and his band of loyal musicians and opera performers have been at it each summer for the last forty-two years. Max helped wear out the original 1906 pavilion, and before the open-air promenade with the extravagantly leaky roof was replaced a couple of years ago, his productions were frequently rained upon but never out.

In addition to the Sunday afternoon park pops, Max and his St. Paul Opera Workshop have been doing summer-evening musicals in the promenade for almost two decades. Max leans toward such Rodgers and Hammerstein productions as *Carousel, Oklahoma,* and *The King and I,* which he and his production crew manage to boil into a single, profusely simple scene generally featuring a painting of a tree, depicting a forest, and a castle/cottage/shop/inn door that actually opens and shuts. One day recently, Max was patrolling the stage in Bermuda shorts, supervising the hinging of The Door so it could become part of the *Carousel* set. Something caused him to chuckle. No, make that cackle.

"We were doing *Sweethearts* by Victor Herbert one summer, and the scene was in front of the 'Laundry of the White Geese,' for which we had an appropriately illustrated sign. At the time, there were a thousand ducks sitting on Como Lake, and we were quite used to their quacking. But right in the middle of the song, 'Jeanette and Her Wooden Shoes,' a huge white goose walked up on stage, looked at the sign, and began squawking. She finally ambled off, at her own speed, and it brought the house down."

The goose would be considered a natural element, and all of nature's elements are part of Max's performances. A lusty, wet storm out of the East one Sunday pushed all the spectators up onto the stage with the orchestra. Since there was no room left to play, the musicians put the instruments away and mingled until the storm died down. Then the audience wiped off their benches, sat down, and the show resumed.

"The only thing that would stop us is a tornado," said Max. He almost played through one once and paused only when park officials evacuated the pavilion.

"He would have kept right on playing if they hadn't told him to stop," said Max's wife, Lil.

Maximilian Metzger was born in Germany in 1922, the only son of Ludwig Metzger and Mady Metzger-Zeigler, a mezzo-soprano of international reputation. The family came to the United States in 1931, and Ludwig took over management of the old Deutsches Haus (German House) on Rice Street, which became the American House early in World War II.

And Mady became St. Paul's first lady of song, cracking Broadway at the age of sixty-two with a hit performance in Carnegie Hall. She was known in other concert halls from Vienna to Milan to Munich, but St. Paul was her beloved home, and she founded the St. Paul Opera Workshop, which Max took over upon her death in 1979.

He inherited from his mother, he said, her all-consuming passion for music but not her voice. He was a boy soprano with an Episcopal youth choir, but when his voice changed, his mother warned him never, ever, to sing another note.

"And if I did," said Max, "I was warned not to claim any relationship with her."

When he was very young, one of Mady's friends was the famous, ferocious Mathilda Heck, the music teacher who terrorized—and taught—generations of St. Paul schoolchildren. Miss Heck dragged "Mox," as she called him, to a Young People's concert performance of the Minneapolis Symphony Orchestra at Northrop Auditorium, and he was intrigued with the strange-looking and sounding pipe hidden in the middle of the orchestra. Miss Heck took him backstage after the performance, where he met the owner of the instrument and learned all about it.

When Max went home, he said, "Mommy, I want a bassoon."

So Max got his bassoon and became a musician, first with the St. Paul Civic Opera Workshop and then, for seven seasons, with a symphony orchestra in Duluth. Along the line, he got to direct the Civic Opera orchestra—and his mother—at the old St. Paul Auditorium.

If Max inherited the music from his mother, he inherited daydreaming from his father. Max has run the Opera Workshop for many decades but said, "I'd be a very poor businessman. The people I work with, thank God, do that, for which I'm very grateful."

"He's a daydreamer," agreed Lil, the second woman in Max's life. Lil, who's known him since the 1940s and who'd sung with the Opera Workshop as a member of the chorus, married Max in 1980, accepting all of Max's little eccentricities such as the fact that he has never driven a car ("He has his head in the clouds," said Lil. "He'd probably hit something.") So Max and Lil take a cab or bus wherever they go.

"He loves to walk around downtown," said Lil. "He knows so many people, and so many he doesn't know come up and say they enjoy his music."

Some of them wind up on stage, singing for Max. One of those was former Mayor George Latimer, who harbors a not-so-secret fantasy of being an opera star. Max had George sing "Shine on Harvest Moon."

"There's not too much I could do to screw up that song," said Latimer. "After I was through, and every time I'd see Max, he'd say, 'Thank you and bless you for all you've done.' It made me wonder what I'd done for him."

Max said that to everyone; "Bless you for all you've done." And many of his associates have been accepting his blessings for decades, including saxophonist Harlan Ebbert, who's played for him for forty years, longtime drummer Connie Villars, and lead Irish tenor and now Opera Workshop managing director Jerry Lanahan.

"He's a sweet man," said Lanahan, "but he also has a temper that shows if he doesn't get what he wants. His ultimate weapon is to threaten us all with his singing if we don't obey. I'd say he either sounds like a bullfrog or a man who's suddenly straddled a picket fence."

Whatever Max does, it works. His free pops concerts fill the promenade each summer Sunday afternoon with from five hundred to seven hundred spectators, and the first Opera Workshop production this summer, of *Barefoot in the Park,* was such a financial success that the workshop donated fifteen hundred dollars back to the city.

"The beauty of it," said Max, "is that I get to do what I love doing. There is nowhere else I'd rather be than directing music in the lakeside pavilion at Como Park in St. Paul. I've not missed a thing. I've got Lil, I've got my work, I've got my friends, I've got enough to get by.

"And bless you for all you've done."

Breakfast with Betty

JUNE 5, 1999

"Want some coffee?"

The bearded stranger on the other side of the U-shaped counter passed me a cup, then filled it with Betty's coffee. Another one of Betty's early-morning clients was reading a column I'd written about old airplane hangars, so everybody at the counter talked aviation for a while.

Betty's Cafe, on Concord Street in South St. Paul, is where the new customer can't possibly be left out of conversation. The place is about the size of a one-and-a-half-car Sussel garage, and everybody faces everybody else—and Betty Harren as she patrols the infield, setting out her homemade maple syrup and trading sassy one-liners with her guests.

"What'll you have?" she asked.

How about breakfast special number two?

"Those cakes are big. How about breakfast number one? Two eggs, toast, two sausages, and hash browns."

OK.

"And I'll give you one cake. You have to try the cakes. I make my own syrup."

The boys in trucks, vans, cars, and on Harleys are pulling up to the nondescript, formerly white stucco, flat-roofed building. The Harley rider gets this from Betty:

"With your hours, you could do my dishes for me."

She had so many customers one day, the Harley guy jokes, that he just got up, went out in her kitchen, and began washing the dishes.

"That went on for a year and a half, and I was even taking orders from the customers for Betty."

"Any tips?" the man in the beard asked.

"Yeh," replied the Harley guy. "Get out of the business."

So we talked about the high price of Harleys for a while, all the customers around the twenty-stool lunch counter.

"Funny thing," said Betty. "I very seldom get women in here. Most of the people are men, and I like that. Men are so easy to wait on. They never complain about an order."

One day, said Gerry Ensign, a woman did come in, and she started rearranging the art on Betty's wall, all the photos of Betty's two sons, Dick and Larry, and her six grandchildren and her one great-grandchild.

"Betty didn't say anything while the woman was here,"

said Gerry, body shop manager at Fury Motors next door to the little cafe, "and when she left, Betty just put all the art back the way it was."

One day, another regular said, a young fellow and a girl came in and said they wanted fries and burgers.

"Betty said, 'I won't do fries, and I don't do burgers. You want a burger, Burger King is just down the street.'"

"I'll do a hamburger," Betty said, "but nothing fried in grease. I don't fry anything in grease in here. I've been here all these years myself, and I haven't gained any weight."

Betty's been at 720 North Concord Street for thirty-five years, and even though business is not what it was when Concord was a big-deal street, when the packinghouses were in operation and the federal meat inspectors school was right next door, Betty has no plans to quit any time soon. From 5:30 A.M. to 3:00 P.M., five days a week, Betty, a widow in her early eighties, is behind her counter for breakfast and lunch.

The windows in the back of Betty's Cafe look out over the Burlington Northern Santa Fe tracks that pass by at the bottom of a steep slope. A few years back, Betty had a stout rope tied around a tree on the brow of the slope so the railroaders could crawl up to her place.

"I even had the king of hobos in here once," Betty said. "I think it was old Steamtrain Maurie himself. He was such a nice guy."

So the railroaders in the cafe talk about hobos for awhile and about Iowa Blackie, a hobo I know who comes into town regularly on the tracks below Betty's.

"I just lost one of my favorite customers," said Betty. "That was Freddy. He'd been coming in here for thirty years, and now he's gone. That's the hardest thing, to lose your customers . . ."

"Why are you selling your Harley?" one of the regulars asked the Harley guy.

"My wife can't ride it anymore," Harley guy replied. "She's getting old."

"Don't they make trailers for those things?" the regular asked, adding "the bike, not your wife."

"I don't really know why more women don't come in here," Betty said again. "But the guys are so easy to serve."

The Harley guy was telling a joke. "What goes, 'Tick, tick, woof, woof'?" he asks. Nobody at the counter knew.

"A watch dog."

"A watch dog! You get out here and make some coffee for me," Betty ordered.

"Yes, ma'am," said Harley guy, heading for her kitchen. "If I don't do it, I'm in big trouble."

"These have really been happy, happy years," Betty said. "I used to have all my groceries trucked in, but now I buy all of the food myself. And everything is baked and made right here. Pie, lasagna, everything."

Gerry Ensign is there every day for lunch. His favorite is Betty's macaroni-and-ground-beef hot dish.

"And her banana cream pie. But the only way I'll get that is if I bring Betty the bananas. Then I'll get banana cream pie."

═══════

Tending the Lift Bridge

AUGUST 23, 1992

The way Walt DeYoung told it, the excursion boat got his attention first because of the strange way it was progressing downriver. It was headed smack dab for Walt's bridge, which inspired Walt to begin lifting the structure.

The next thing Walt noticed was the siren of an approaching ambulance. The driver told Walt on the police radio that he needed to cross the bridge because there was a highway on the other side that was strewn with human bodies.

To make Walt's evening shift a more memorable one, the excursion boat by then had lost most of its power. The wind had come up on the St. Croix River and was pushing the paddle-wheel boat downstream at a refreshing clip. The ambulance driver, meanwhile, was rounding the last corner on the Stillwater side of the bridge at a brisk rate of speed and urgently asking why the bridge was still up. On top of that, channel sixteen on Walt's marine-band radio was going out.

Walt's stirring soliloquy was interrupted as he paused for breath. His bridge stories require animation, so he was prancing around like Robert Preston singing "There's trouble right here in River City" from *The Music Man*.

He went on, "'Close that bridge!' I'm hearing. 'Keep it open!' I'm hearing. There's a hundred people on the boat, God knows how many bodies scattered out on the highway, and I have to do something. What do I do?"

I wanted to suggest that maybe Walt should have slipped over to Brine's for a bowl of chowder, but no: The man is a dedicated, honorable bridge tender. He stayed at his post, began lowering the bridge as quickly as he could, and used a battery-powered loud-hailer to tell the skipper of the excursion boat to either drop the hook or run his craft onto the beach until the lift went up again.

Walt's shift that night, as it turned out, passed with minimal carnage. All nights on the Stillwater Bridge are not like that, of course. Some nights, Walt just gets mooned.

"These two guys were coming across the bridge in a pickup truck. I looked away for just a short moment and then back at the truck, and I was looking at the ugliest man in the world. I was wondering how a man's face could get so ugly, and the truck passed the bridge house. The passenger had to have been a contortionist because he'd slipped out of his trousers and done a somersault in the front seat. He had a cap on top of his butt, and there it all was, looking straight at me as the truck went by. I'd have to call that one a full moon. Then, of course, there are the times the girls go by and I get busted. . . . "

Walt DeYoung and the old Stillwater lift bridge make a good pair: two charming, barnacled relics of a time when two lanes were plenty. But now a new, wider, higher bridge is imminent, which opens the question of what will become of Walt and the old bridge. It's a problem that seems to be heading Walt's way as surely as the confluence of that excursion boat and that ambulance.

Long before the onset of his bridge-tending career, Walt was in the U.S. Air Force, where he once attended a lecture on nuclear warfare during which enlisted men were encouraged to ask questions.

"Since they wanted to hear from me, I stood up and said, 'Sir, I think this is insane. Sir.'

"My life in the air force changed dramatically after that. I didn't have much of a future in nuclear warfare, so they made me a gridiron gladiator. I'm still getting one hundred dollars a month for my service-connected football injury."

Sometime later, he became a union organizer in New Jersey. Walt gave a wry wink that made him look like Walter Matthau plotting something and said, "The ladies' garment workers union offered a swift education."

He took his union job as an organizer so seriously that the dark suits from management called him in for consultation. He learned that one can accomplish a great deal in East Coast labor work if one is able to utter the words, "Please don't do this thing to me."

Walt had trouble with phrases like that, so he wound up in northern Minnesota in a cabin near Bemidji far from those people who wanted to do those things to him.

Walt and the Stillwater lift bridge eventually found each other six or seven years ago, two colorful artifacts, and now there's talk of both of them retiring.

Walt's a seasonal employee of the Minnesota Department of Transportation, working nights and weekends. He's well into his sixties now, and there are other organizing jobs to be done. He's leading the movement to preserve the Chisago County Courthouse, and there's a rest home in Wisconsin that needs to be saved from a real-estate developer. Walt's got some fight left in him, he wants you to know, but the fights don't get any easier.

The bridge is a year younger than Walt, and its work doesn't get any easier, either. It carries sixteen thousand vehicles a day now, and a bridge between the two states at Stillwater, Minnesota, and Houlton, Wisconsin, will have to carry thirty thousand vehicles a day in ten years. The two-lane lift bridge was not built for loads like that, and traffic backups through Stillwater and into the hills of western Wisconsin have stopped being charming for most nearby residents and commuters.

The route for a new, fixed platform bridge near Stillwater has been chosen after years of planning and hearings. It is generally accepted that Wisconsin would be linked to Minnesota by a bridge that would follow Highway 36 straight across the river near NSP's Allen S. King power plant.

All that has been missing for years has been the decision either to go or not go, and even with a new high-volume interstate bridge in operation, an estimated eleven thousand vehicles per day would still use the lift bridge.

And somewhere along the line, the lift bridge acquired a degree of immunity—it got placed on the National Register of Historic Places. Tearing the bridge down would be akin to selling a national park. So the fight has yet to be fought on the future of the lift bridge, which has the distinction of being the last originally constructed lift bridge in the state of Minnesota (the Aerial Bridge in Duluth was originally a fixed bridge).

In the meantime, Walt stops traffic and lifts the bridge on the half hour between 6:00 and 10:00 P.M. in the summer. If you were waiting for the bridge to reopen after a lift on a busy weekend day, you'd think the machinery was intolerably slow. But the lift cycle is actually quite swift: The bridge is up and down in four minutes, about the same amount of time you'll wait for a traffic light at Larpenteur and Snelling near the fairgrounds.

Warning lights begin flashing, then the barriers are lowered, and then the bridge goes up. It's a simple operation, but when the lights begin flashing, someone often tries to beat the lift. One evening it was a motorist in a new conversion van who ignored the bells and flashing lights and suddenly found herself between two lowered arms. She pumped the brakes, looked terrified, and continued across the bridge in a tortured crawl with both fists in her mouth.

"She's gonna run the light," Walt said, providing color commentary. "Here she comes, there she is, Hello, ma'am, go ahead, you're all right now, there she goes, she almost hit the bridge, she's sucking wind now, and now she's across . . . "

People hit the bridge all the time. It's like they come here from all over the state either to hit the bridge or drive off the road on the Wisconsin end of it and plow into the river. Not long ago, a seventy-four-year-old man clipped off one of the arms and ruined his car.

Once in a while, they come to the bridge to jump off. One night, Walt got a call on his radio from the excursion boat *Andiamo*.

"Someone's going to jump, Walt. They're up on your bridge."

"Get that?" said Walt. "Suddenly, it's *my* bridge. So I went out, and sure enough, right at the top of one of the towers, there's a young guy. He had that look on his face like he's really going to do it. I told him to come down, and he just swore at me and said he was going to die.

"I don't know what to do, but I'm stalling for time. I told him, 'It's your decision, and I won't try to talk you out of it. But please don't do it on my time. Do me a favor and wait another half-hour because it'll be someone else's shift then. If you jump on my shift, I'll have to clean you up.'

"I'm telling this guy what a mess he's going to make. 'Your brains are going to splatter, and then your liver, your kidneys, your spleen, your heart, your lungs, your gall bladder'—I'm mentioning every organ in his body—'your stomach is going to splatter, and all your (bleep).' I had him thinking about how awful he was going to look, and he got so mad at me that he came down from the bridge and chased me uptown."

Walt was standing on the roadway of the bridge in the soft summer twilight. He raised the bridge to its limits—fifty-one feet above the water—and signaled the *Andiamo* and several assorted smaller craft to proceed through.

The bridge's ups and downs are signaled with horns and bells. There may be more disciplined lift bridge operators around but not many as cordial as Walt. The one official signal in his repertoire is "Beep, beep, beep-beep-beep," and then he waits for the boat to finish it off with a "boop-boop."

"I don't lift for antennas, though," he said. Sometimes, when the river's really high, he does lift for ducks. "Insistent ducks."

Walt has just enough time at the top to contemplate the town, the river, and all the little boats that've come to catch the concert in the park at the foot of the bridge.

"I'm in love with this bridge," he said. "This is a job for a philosopher, you know. If you aren't a philosopher when you get here, you'll become one after a few cold nights out here by yourself in October. I tell you, this bridge can get chilly when the wind whips down the river valley. It can be just like a storm on the North Atlantic sometimes."

I asked Walt if the bridge is haunted, and he said of course it is. I asked him if there are monsters in the river, and he looked at me as though I'd dropped a log on his toe.

Of course there are monsters in the river, Walt said. There's this strange wake that doesn't follow a boat. It just appears out in calm water from time to time and then goes zigging across the river. If it's a fish, Walt said, it's a monster, a behemoth.

Something else about that river. A body was fished out next to the bridge last year. As the body was being taken from the river, the wind suddenly tore down the valley and sent shivers up Walt's back. Then, it just as suddenly got calm, until a hearse came along for the body. While the body was being loaded, the wind once again ripped down through the valley.

"I came into the bridge house and locked the door. I stayed inside until my shift was over."

Two young people were peddling their bikes across the bridge on the pedestrian side. They stopped across from the lift house, and when Walt rang the signals for a lift, the young man asked if they could stay on the part of the bridge that would be lifted.

"Sorry, son," said Walt. "Not since that woman got cut in half up here." The two cyclists leave rubber marks getting off the bridge.

"Did that really happen?" I asked Walt.

"Of course," he said. "Would a bridge tender lie?"

No One Made Better Ice

DECEMBER 15, 1998

My hand still aches from the last time he gripped it in that vise of his, that bricklayer's hand of concrete and steel. If you knew Wes, you knew that grip of his and the unblinking eye of the eagle as he took you in tow. That grip was not a test of your strength by Wes, but his way of saying how very, very pleased he was to see you.

The East Side held its breath and said its prayers for Wes Barrette last week after word got around quickly about the terrible head injury he sustained in a fall while on the ice, with his boys, at Harding Arena. He suffered irreversible brain damage, dying on Sunday, four days after the mishap, and I could not write this unless I knew it to be true: There was not another person on the entire East Side of St. Paul any more loved, trusted, or respected than hockey coach Wes Barrette.

There was another Wes Barrette greeting. The whisker

rub. Generations of hockey players are nodding right now, remembering what it was like to be given Wes's ultimate seal of approval.

"I couldn't wait to grow up, get whiskers, and give Wes a rub," said Mike Schwartz, one of Wes's boys from the Midget teams of 1973 and 1974. Mike and his three brothers all played on Wes Barrette hockey teams, and now Mike is head hockey coach at Augsburg College.

The Schwartz brothers and their cousin Chris, who is my son, were among the hundreds of young men who played for Wes in his forty-five years of coaching youth hockey and building citizenship through hard work, loyalty, respect, and love.

"I don't have a lot of rules," I heard Wes say to his East Side Midgets on the night Chris made his team. "But there are four: There's no drinking on my team, no smoking on my team, no cussing, and I don't ever want to hear anyone say, 'My old man' or 'My old lady.'"

"Wes didn't just take the cream of the crop," recalls his assistant coach, Steve Spock. "Some of the kids had gotten cut from their high school teams, some were kids that other coaches didn't want, kids who'd gotten into trouble, kids from troubled homes. He gave them all a chance, and he gave them love."

Steve played hockey for Wes back in the 1960s and has coached Midget and Junior Gold hockey (high school level) with him since 1973. The simple values of hard work and love, Steve said, were Wes Barrette hallmarks. Values, prayer on the bench before a game—often led by the players themselves— and Wes's old kangaroo-hide skates with old-fashioned, tube-steel blades. Everyone else in the world was skating on plastic, and Wes was still wearing his old metal blades.

Wes's coaching was centered around Hayden Heights, a little playground in the northeast corner of the city. I showed up about twenty-five years ago to help coach the Hayden Heights Mites, beginner's hockey, and one of the first things I learned was how to make ice, Barrette-style.

No one made better ice in the days when some hockey programs were actually run out of doors. Wes would be the nozzle man, waving the working end of the hose around like a maestro conducting a Sousa march.

Making outdoor ice is almost a lost art, but for Wes the ritual of shoveling the rink and flooding was important conditioning, and it called for teamwork that helped unite his boys, who came from all over town. When they were through, those who made ice got pie and coffee at a White Bear Avenue restaurant.

"We used to love to go to his house and just hang out," said Mike Schwartz. "His wife, Aud (Audrey), helped us sort out our girl problems."

Wes and his big blue Chevy truck were a familiar sight on the East Side and at its hockey rinks and arenas. He was born in St. Paul, lived on the East Side all his life, and was a superb football player at Johnson High School. He won All-City honors as left halfback in 1945 and was a member of the school's Hall of Fame.

Wes was seventy when he died at St. John's Hospital in Maplewood. He was survived by Audrey, son Neal, daughters Cheryl Malark of White Bear Lake and Paula Schulze of St. Paul, and six grandchildren.

Neal and Wes worked together as stonemasons and bricklayers for many years, and their most recent job was the most beautiful, Neal said: a home with a thirty-five-foot-tall natural fieldstone chimney. They weren't quite through with it when Wes was injured, and Neal went back and forth between the job and the hospital, finally finishing the stonework Monday before making arrangements for his father's funeral.

"I had to finish it," said Neal. "For Wessie. He'd want it done, and when the capstone is set on the very top of the chimney, I'm going back to carve his name in it."

One other thing is being done to honor Wes. His funeral was at Gustavus Adolphus Lutheran Church on the East Side, and visitation was at the Crestwood Park Mortuary on White

Bear Avenue. Wes's big blue truck was parked out front at both places. His hockey stick and his old kangaroo-hide skates were there in the cab.

Facing the Storms on Lake Superior

JULY 3, 1993

The storms that howl in from the northeast and send Lake Superior into rage, those great, seething, screaming storms that pick the lake up like a boiling pot and hurl it all around, are not the ones that cause Walter Sve to flinch. Northeasters are the blows that bellow and grunt and lumber in like sumo wrestlers and rip the siding off the cabins, rearrange the beach rock, and mesmerize the tourists.

Rather, it is the northwester that Walter fears, the storm that sneaks its dark little nose over the steep North Shore hills to his back. These are the quiet, hostile brutes that puff once and pounce. The northwester is the sudden, ruthless demon that comes out of nowhere and kills Lake Superior sailors who are not fast enough.

Walter Sve goes out on Lake Superior at sunrise each morning, one and one-half miles offshore to tend the herring nets he's set in 450 feet of water. He used to go as far as seven miles out, to 1,000 feet of water, but maybe he just doesn't feel fast enough anymore.

Walter told stories of the lake recently as we pulled his herring net from twelve fathoms (seventy-two feet) of water. One day, several years ago, he was seven miles out, had emptied his nets quickly because he did not like the way the northwest sky looked, and set out into the building seas for shore. The sky over the hills suddenly showed black, and the monster was atop him. He knew his family would have seen it, too, and would be watching from the shore, just like in the painting by

Howard Sivertsen of the Isle Royal family and its vigil on the shore.

"You cannot run fast," said Walter. "You have to give the boat a chance to catch up with the sea. That is when the shape of the boat is important, and the weight. You must not have a boat that is too straight or flat. The boat must have belly to it."

Walter made it back, but a trip that normally took eighteen minutes took more than an hour that day. He had another story about the northwest wind. On Palm Sunday in 1935, two young men went out on the lake in their shirtsleeves because it was sunny and sixty degrees. Then the monster came over the hill from the northwest, plunging the temperature forty degrees in an hour.

The men might have made it home had they not lost their engine, but ten days later, their boat, with their bodies lashed to it, washed ashore at Cornucopia, Wisconsin, twenty-six miles to the east. That is how Walter's wife, Carol, lost her father and her uncle.

So even on bluebird days, Walter watches the compass mounted in the bow of the *Tern*, the eighteen-foot, cedar-and-fir boat that brings him to his herring nets each day. He goes out to the northeast, so he must return to the southwest. Most mornings are clear, and from one and one-half miles, he can still see his landmarks: the concrete-filled docks in front of the large, gray boathouse he and his father built and, higher on the hill, the home of his brother, Leonard. Fog and rain can close in quickly, though, from any direction and turn the horizon into white gauze. Lake Superior fishermen have been found dead in their boats after a storm, sitting upright, their bodies turned to ice in their mackinaws and their hands frozen to the oars—silent testimony that they simply could not get back.

That Lake Superior is both beautiful and treacherous is no revelation. Since the advent of American shipping in 1835, more than three hundred vessels have been lost to its caprice, its reefs that come out of nowhere, and its awful fog. Walter and Carol Sve run Split Rock Cabins at the mouth of the Split Rock River. It was there, in 1905, that the new 478-foot steamship ore freighter, the *William Edenborn*, went aground, burying her bow in the shore woods in a blinding, nighttime November storm. Her tow, the 436-foot ore barge *Madeira*, drifted out of control up the shoreline after the towline broke, eventually running aground and breaking up at the foot of Split Rock Lighthouse.

The lake, over the years, has claimed thousands of seamen —few shipwrecked sailors survive the brutally cold waters, and the lake rarely gives up its dead—but the toll from the *Edenborn* and *Madeira* wrecks was one each; sailors who were lost when they tried to scramble ashore through the rampaging surf. One is said to have died when he tried to leap from a swaying mast to a rocky cliff over the lake.

The *Edenborn* probably ran aground on a low rock just off Walter's shore, a couple of little bumps sticking out of the water that he calls Split Rock Island. Many years ago, Walter's father, Ragnvald, dragged ashore a five-foot chunk of rusting iron that still rests on the beach near Walter's boathouse. It was one of the blades from the *Edenborn*'s propeller, snapped off when the ship grounded.

Walter is sixty-five and carries on at Split Rock much as his father did after he came to America from Norway in 1927 and married Ragnhild. Walter's father died in 1988, but his mother, who is eighty-five, still lives in the big, white family home near the shore. Walter chuckles when he thinks of how he started on the lake, in a boat that was powered by oar. At first, his mother would row for his father, who would tend his nets. Walter and his sister, Verna May, rode along because they couldn't be left on shore. When they were old enough, the children each got an oar. Eventually, each child was big enough to handle both oars. Walter began fishing commercially in 1944 and remembers bringing in as many as twenty-two hundred pounds of herring in one load.

"I began pulling nets at 6:00 A.M. and came ashore at

3:00 P.M.," he said. "Sixteen herring boxes were full, and the fish spilled out into the boat. That, I believe, was my best day."

These days, Walter nets twenty-five or thirty-five pounds of herring, occasionally one hundred or two hundred pounds when fishing is really good. There are only a couple of dozen fishermen licensed to take herring from the North Shore, and Walter sells as much as he can catch to nearby restaurants at Beaver Bay and Gooseberry Falls.

The herring fishing has returned in the last few years to Lake Superior after a dry spell that lasted all the twenty-five years that Reserve Mining Company discharged its taconite tailings into the lake at Silver Bay, just up the shore from Split Rock. Walter complained about not being able to see lake bottom through the turbidity soon after the discharge began in 1955, but it was not until May 1980 that the daily discharge of sixty-seven thousand tons of mining waste was finally halted as the result of one of the longest, most complex and most important environmental lawsuits in North America's history.

Walter's four-hundred-foot herring gill net is stretched like a submerged belt seventy-two feet beneath the surface, spring to fall. He is also one of only eight North Shore fishermen who are permitted by the Minnesota Department of Natural Resources to take up to three hundred lake trout each year in May and September. In exchange for that privilege, Walter reports on the fish: their size, whether they bear scars from the lamprey suckers, and whether the trout are native or stocked (stocked fish have clipped fins).

"I make enough to pay for gas," Walter said. He also does it out of love for the lake and affection for his boat, the *Tern*, a black-and-red, wood-strip boat that has belonged to the Sves since 1939. It has been an open boat since the day Walter and his father were fishing and a gale out of the northwest threw a wave at them that carried the cabin away.

The *Tern*'s four-cylinder Graymarine engine powers the boat out to the fishing grounds with all appropriate dignity but very little speed. When Walter must get on the lake and off with some urgency, he launches the long, high-sided, flat-bottomed, plywood and fiberglass boat he built. That's the boat powered by "Big Ole," a 1965 twenty-eight-horsepower Evinrude. A spare "kicker" outboard engine is always stowed on either of the boats he takes out.

He also carries—reluctantly—survival suits, $350.00 rubber coveralls designed to keep him alive should he or a passenger go into the lake. It's a Coast Guard requirement that he thinks is futile. In a test, it took him ten minutes to put on the suit, and he couldn't get his hands, substantial fisherman's hands that they are, into the glove ends. If his boat were in trouble, he said, he wouldn't have those ten minutes to spare.

He shrugged. If that is what is required, though, he'll carry the survival suits.

Walter and Carol have four children, three sons and a daughter. His youngest son, Eric Christopher, wants to take over the cabins when the time comes.

I watched as Walter neatly fileted the herring he would sell to the restaurants for $2.50 per pound and asked if he thinks he's missed anything important in life. Walter thought about it for a while before replying.

"We flew to Norway in 1980 on one of those 747s. I couldn't believe all the people they put on that plane.

"No. I don't think I've missed anything. There is nowhere else that I would want to be."

*A Small Town
on the Prairie*

Jake the Drake at Pelican Lake

MAY 9, 1990

There's a little bit of a curve in Highway 82 as it rides a ridge on the east edge of Pelican Lake near the Ashby Motel where Jake the Drake works one night a year. Last Friday afternoon, a Chev Suburban whistled off the road there, just missed a big cottonwood tree, and stopped a few feet shy of Stosh Moran's beached ice house. The next night, a lady shot the curve in her pickup truck and went off the road on the other side, clipping off a power pole about hip-boot high.

I wasn't sure how much more of this excitement I could take, but none of it mattered to Jake the Drake as he was paraded out like a gladiator to his low, chicken-wire pen with numbers one to one hundred painted on its floor. Jake had dined well on corn for a couple of days, and just before his twilight performance, he had a good slug of lake water. He was deposited with some ceremony on the numbered surface. For a moment, all of Ashby could not have been more still if Jake had been mighty Casey at the bat. The big goose waddled around, checking out his favorite numbers. Then, oblivious to his mesmerized audience of humans, Jake the Drake shrugged and decorated square number eighty-two, making a young man who had temporarily bought the space richer by a five-hundred-dollar goose gun.

Jake's nonchalant performance was the usual prelude to the annual Coots Unlimited soiree in the quiet little part of central Minnesota between Alexandria and Fergus Falls. This was the eleventh year that sportsmen in Grant, Douglas, and Ottertail Counties have honored the dumb but lovable coot (a mudhen) with a big outdoor party that has raised more than a quarter of a million dollars for area wildlife projects.

As usual, more than six hundred people from such places as Carlos, Dalton, Evansville, Elbow Lake, Brandon, Battle

Lake, Fergus Falls, Alexandria, the Twin Cities, towns as far away as Iowa, and, of course, tiny Ashby dropped in at Galen Boerhave's motel and resort to celebrate spring under a couple of big revival tents. They arrived by the busload, attracted by barbecued buffalo, smoked carp, twenty-five-cent beer, and an opportunity to hit it big on the door prizes and raffles. Dozens of quality shotguns and rifles and fishing, camping, and boating gear are donated each year by area sponsors.

I've become a regular, because I can't think of another place in the whole world where you can win a mallard's-head toilet plunger. Son Chris joined me for the first time this year and was dazzled by the prize selection of huge fish coolers, tents, sleeping bags, framed sports prints by famous wildlife artists, and expensive outdoor toys.

Son Chris won a frozen turkey breast.

Each year, I wait for someone to claim Belgaard's Buffalo, a huge, shaggy, mounted head that gets raffled off. But for the fourth year, its winner took the two-hundred-dollar alternative offer. She really wanted the big buffalo head, said Pam, of Anoka, but she'd never get it home in her Subaru. She wouldn't have gotten it home in a moving van.

This mellow little festival on the shore of a lake out on the prairie is what Minnesota does best, and by the next day, you'd never know there'd been a big party or that an announcer, at one point, had really said, "You do not have to be present to win. If you're already gone, please tell someone."

Just another day in paradise.

Ice House Plows into a Plymouth

FEBRUARY 18, 1994

We did not set out to go ice fishing with Stosh and Buddy, but that's what happened. And I'd like to announce that Stosh's ice house is a step up from the inside of his old El Camino, which is where he keeps the goose decoys and his Sunday wardrobe.

He calls the house his shack, but his place is right out of *Better Homes and Gardens*. There are padded deacons benches on either end of the house, wall-to-wall carpeting, built-in cabinets for Stosh's Wild Turkey, plush blue swivel chairs liberated, I would guess, from the Ashby Legion post, and a couple of metal folding chairs that have the church-basement look. Buddy, the big black lab, is not allowed to drink from the sucker bucket.

And Stosh's house is filled with winter sunlight, streaming in through four thermal-pane windows, one of which I am gazing out of as a big steel-sided ice house comes sliding by and squashes a little white car into Stosh's El Camino. You say you've heard of cars hitting ice houses; when was the last time you saw an ice house hit a car?

I go north with my friend J. D. to Ashby for refuge several times a year, for the open-water fishing, the duck hunting, and the people. In the spring, we go to the Coots Unlimited banquet, a very rural version of Ducks Unlimited. In the fall, we sit atop the highest hill in Jimmy Peterson's cornfield at the edge of town, crouching in pits when the geese come over. From the hilltop, you can see some of the other fields where we've hunted geese with Stosh and his father, George.

Stosh is quiet in his ice house when J. D. and I stop to visit. George is not well, and the funeral for our young friend Marcia has just been held at the Lutheran church in town. Gopher Johnson died this winter, and Jack Nelson, too. There is not much to celebrate here: The fish are not biting, and Buddy is being a pain in the butt. But the sun is out, and Stosh's pal, Johnny, comes calling in his new, little, white Plymouth, which he parks behind the El Camino.

We talk about geese and bluebills in big flocks. We talk about fishing for walleyes come spring and how good it was last year right around the corner in the Narrows. We talk about big black crappies that used to school up in Widow's Bay and off Indian Mound, and we wonder if they'll ever be back the way they once were.

It's turning out to be not so bad an afternoon. Then, we hear a loud rumbling sound. I look out the window just in time to see a big snowplow go by, towing an icehouse that looks to be about a six-holer. The house swings wide, bashing into Johnny's car and launching it into the old El Camino, which has real bumpers and does not budge. The front of the little white car crumbles like a soda cracker.

"Now why do you suppose he did that?" Johnny asked. "That's my new car!" We pile out of Stosh's house onto the ice. Buddy wants a piece of that truck driver.

"I guess we ought to exchange names and numbers," said Johnny.

"I don't know why," answered the truck driver. "We're cousins."

A Prairie Home Halloween

OCTOBER 30, 1994

Off in a corner by himself, doing God knows what and not moving at all, was Beaver Johnson from up by Lake Christina. Beaver didn't say much, so people automatically thought he was old Bullhead from right here in Ashby. Beaver had a hard time getting in the front door because, under normal circumstances, an ice-fishing house doesn't walk too far.

The tooth fairies both had red beards bordering on pink and went about three hundred pounds apiece. They flitted about in their long underwear and frilly tutus, anointing people with their dainty little magic wands and chirping, "Riches will follow, riches will follow."

Wolfman lurched around in his checked Pendleton shirt,

sucking beer out of a long-necked bottle through a straw.

The bashful wench in the white brocade shawl had a set of choppers you could use to eat a tomato through a picket fence.

Big, puffy yellow pumpkins bopped around the floor. There were ball players, bag ladies, pirates, rag dolls, puppy dogs, and a nun.

No one really knows how the Halloween costume party at the American Legion post in Ashby got started. A couple of out-of-towners showed up in gorilla costumes one year for the annual volunteer fireman's dance, and ever since then, folks wearing elaborate costumes toodle on in from Melby, Dalton, Evansville, Elbow Lake, Fergus Falls, Millerville, Urbank, Erdahl, Brandon, Alexandria, and, it's fair to suppose, Clontarf or even Murdock.

Ashby does all right for itself, even when it's not celebrating something. About 488 people live here, out on the prairie alongside Interstate 94 between Alexandria and Fergus Falls, where a man by the name of Hill once built a railroad and someone named Kittson built a hotel.

The railroad's gone, the hotel's gone, and the people from the Twin Cities who make decisions for the rest of the state keep talking about killing nine-man football and consolidating rural school districts. Ironically, many Ashby folk think that a particularly strong and popular independent school district and the Ashby Arrows are what keep their town vibrant.

Corn around Ashby is always the big crop. Beans were huge this year, too. Construction of everything from roads to schools is going full-blast, nine-man football still rules, and about half the people in town walk around camouflaged.

Duck and goose hunting on the lakes and in the rolling fields that surround Ashby always have kept the lights from going out early. Pickup trucks around here routinely are occupied by dogs and shotguns, and no one bats an eye when Jimmy Rylander cruises by with his homemade, sit-in goose decoy, which makes him look like a Winter Carnival float.

So the town is full this weekend with hunters from the

Cities, and everyone, it seems, in Grant, Douglas, and Ottertail Counties who owns a rubber mask or a pair of pink nylon
tights.

Over-organization seems never to be a preoccupation in
Ashby. Things just happen here. Coots Unlimited just sort
of grew around a need one time to move an old train depot.
Some of the boys in town gathered, shot a few coot for dinner,
and began an annual ritual.

Coots Unlimited has thrived for almost twenty years with
hog feeds, game dinners, raffles, and a laid-way-back annual
bash in circus tents that dwarfs even the fireman's ball.

So it happens that on the Saturday night preceding Halloween—it's always on the Saturday night preceding Halloween
—the annual costume party occurs out on the prairie. The
costumes start coming out at sundown, showing up for cock-
tails at the Melby Outpost and at Ashby's cultural hot spot,
the Other Guy's Place, where the big drink is olives and 3.2
beer.

Then the party gets to the Legion post, and Paul Ellingson,
chief of the volunteer fire department, and a few judges with
some bottles of wine for the winners just stand by and let the
thing go.

For weeks, Ashbyites have been quietly trying to decide
just who they want to be, what kind of costume will fool even
their spouses. The women seem especially good at it, arriving
together in sullen, protective clumps of Gummi Bears or hags,
their hands gloved so no one—not even their husbands—will
recognize rings or knuckles. Many of them don't speak all
night, firing off notes or simple grunts.

Only when the costumes come off at the end of the night
are the real identities known. A few never do take off their
costumes; some in Ashby take their Halloween fantasies
home with them.

So it occurred last year that a man dressed as a fish house
sort of heaved himself into the Legion club, like a bull walrus
moving up the beach. That was Beaver Johnson. He sat in a

corner by himself most of the night, making noise only when he wanted a beer or when a fish came on his line.

Bill and Hillary Clinton, of course, were there, he of smaller stature than she, and when the masks finally did come off, he was she and she was he.

Troy Nelson came all the way back home from Long Island, New York, for the party, dressing up like a caveman and terrorizing everyone with his hideous gestures.

Curt Thompson and Luke Probst, both of Ashby, pranced about all night as a pair of noisy horsemen on mounts they'd made from a fifty-gallon plastic drum cut in half the long way.

The caveman and the two horses won prizes for the costumes, as did a trio of nurses from the clinic in Alexandria that came as a pair of delivery-room nurses and their patient, a very pregnant witch, who acted out her part with clinical precision.

That witch, the folks at the costume party will remember this year, was Marcia Anderson, who was a lively, enterprising den mother to the whole town. She was one of eighteen friends and relatives that Ashby has buried so far this year at the little cemetery on the south edge of town. Marcia, just forty-two, died in an auto wreck last February, a death that left the entire community in shock because Marcia's energy was what made Ashby an especially close town.

"But the town pulls itself together pretty well in tough times," Paul Ellingson said. "Hard to say what it takes, but we've always done it together."

═══════════

Everybody Needs an Ashby

NOVEMBER 18, 1996

Steward of Things Small Garrison Keillor recently grieved for "little Swede towns" on the far prairie in Minnesota. In a newspaper essay about nostalgia, Keillor characterized small towns as inevitable casualties of the vast metropolitan suburbs.

Death of the little town is not regularly on the agenda when we're hunkered down in the goose pits up in Jimmy Peterson's bean fields behind the high school at Ashby. Nor out at nearby North Pass, which isn't too far from old Smoothglide's pheasant farm, nor out near the Bengston place where we sometimes linger until the sun goes down and the geese stop flying.

There's a big round table at the back of City Restaurant where the regulars roll to see who pays for morning coffee. They talk about the ducks, the corn, and nine-man football, and they talk about when the water was lower and when it was higher. But you don't hear much about this small Swede town out on the western prairie folding.

Ashby is where you watch the comings and goings of Loophole the lawyer and Drano the plumber, Markie the barber, as well as the sheriff, the town cop, and once in a while we've got to go see Gladys the duck lady out by the county line and to check on the new stuff at Ostrom's store near Dalton. That's as busy as it ought to get.

I've not talked about small-town destiny with Stosh Moran, who puts freeway guardrails together for a living and presents really good friends with pint jars of smoked salmon from his Great Lakes fishing trips with Butch and Jimmy Rylander. I've shared the duck blind with Stosh and with Driggins the electrician and our old friend Andy the gas truck driver, and there's just not enough time to talk about this horrid business of small Swedish towns dying on the prairie.

We've talked a lot about our friend Tubby Hoff, who was recently crushed to death by his road grader, and we've talked about George, Stosh's late father, and about how much we miss his magnificent friendship. And when we're done, we sit on tailgates and share our powdered sugar doughnuts with Buddy and Oscar, the old bird dogs. That takes time to do right.

I should report now on the duck hunting this fall at Ashby.

It was not good, but that was not bad. We had lots to slow down for and to talk about.

My friend J. D. and my sons Chris and Erik were delegates to conferences with Andy about how the decoys must be set at sunup in a changing wind and about whether a cormorant has redeeming social value.

I talked with Andy about his Presbyterian church and about his big old white Mercurys. We sat together and wondered where all the ducks were this year and about what happened to Tubby. The mornings go fast when you've got so much to do, and in the afternoons Stosh, J. D., and I toured dirt roads and waved to people, who all waved back. Over at the Other Guy's Place, the beers come in frosted mugs with olives bobbing in them. That may not sound like much, but it's enough.

This little Scandinavian town out on the western prairie was a special place to Leo, who was J. D.'s father. It became a special place to J. D. when he was just a little boy, and it has become an essential refuge for me and for Chris and Erik, who now feel as woven as we do into the fabric of the town.

I do not expect more from this town than that it be there. Custodian Keillor reminded me of how much everyone needs an Ashby.

The Ritual of the Hunt

NOVEMBER 7, 1996

The Minnesota duck hunter could live for about a week on the food left over from the previous year in the pockets of his hunting clothes, and I'm finding crushed Snickers bars and flattened Milky Ways as Buddy, the black Lab with the pitbull-torn ear, digs for a salamander on the floor of Jimmy Peterson's goose pit in the fields west of Ashby.

What Buddy and I are doing may be as much as we get done today, and that's perfectly OK.

On a late October Saturday, we're atop a big hill, and down below, Jimmy Peterson the gentleman farmer cruises slowly west on the county road in his maroon Chevy pickup truck. The old inspector has to make his rounds, and today they might take him as far as Dalton, where his boys are combining beans in the fields above another spot we hunt. A fellow has to check on things like that.

Jimmy's Chevy might go faster than thirty miles an hour, but a fellow just has to take time to check on things and wave to people. The inspector has got a full schedule of slow cruising most days, and he still has to stop by City Restaurant, the co-op, maybe the bank, the Legion, and Markie's barbershop.

My friend J. D. is over on the next hill to the west in Markie's goose pit. The sheriff lined that pit with treated plywood a couple of years ago, and it might be the best wooden, goose-shooting pit in this whole county. It would be a toss-up between that one and the pit shared by Buddy, Stosh Moran, and me, a pit lined with pieces of a big green aluminum sign that used to say "Melrose."

Stosh had something to do with this box burrowed into Jimmy Peterson's wheat field. Buddy is his dog, and Stosh works for one of those companies that install highway signs and guardrails. Things like that all fit together out here on Minnesota's western prairie, where the land gets as hilly as Minnesota land can get before it goes flat on its way to the Dakotas.

The boys at Ashby High have played really good nine-man football this season, our friend Andy tells us, until a playoff loss to Hillcrest ended their great season.

On other fall mornings, we lounge behind the cattails on the south side of our lake out by Dalton. We sit on old plastic buckets on the grassy shore there, hidden by the tall brush. We've set bluebill and redhead decoys out in the water downwind from us, and there's quite a few of them to keep our eyes on, so we get started. We watch the sky and we watch the decoys, for hours. Slowly.

There's important work like that to be done here in Ashby, and sometimes it doesn't all get done in a day, so we have to come back, and come back again. We've been doing that all fall. Now we face the prospect of ice forming on our decoys. The sloughs and the small lakes freeze first, and finally the big lakes slam shut by late November.

Each fall we come here to wait for the sun in the crisp, dark mornings and talk with Stosh and with Steve, with Andy and Denny and Jimmy and Butch and Markie and all our other friends.

From up in Jimmy Peterson's goose pits we can see the high school where the game was played Friday. There is Pelican Lake to the south and the points we fish for their walleye early in the year. We can see Frog Lake, and there are stories that will be told about that place and old Tubby Hoff. We see the hills and the woods we hunted many years ago with Stosh's late dad, George. We'll talk about George, sweet, lovely George, and the stories will make everyone feel good.

From up here in these pits we see the red combines climb across the hills, chewing at the beans. The mailman, Jimmy Rylander, goes by with the duck boat sticking out of his truck and blows his goose call at us. We see Driggins, the electrician, go by with his old, deaf yellow Lab, Oscar, who likes our powdered sugar doughnuts. Markie the barber might come by, and, of course, Jimmy Peterson, the inspector.

There's a thousand Canada geese in the air, sailing with the wind out of the East, then clawing their way toward some southern place. We might annoy one or two of them from our little pits on the hill. That's why we're here, but not really.

Here's to Buddy

We lost Buddy several weeks ago. That big, tough, cantankerous black Lab slipped a little more away from us each weekend this fall, and even though he still loved to sit in the tall weeds and cattails with all his hunters, it became clear that Buddy's time had come.

Buddy could have been named Bull, or Bear, because he was just as easy to control as either of those beasts. From the time Buddy was a pup, he seemed to know that if he'd just pull a little harder, dig a little deeper, chew a little longer, things would eventually go his way.

The litter that Buddy came from was an interesting one. There was Buddy, and he became partner to Stosh Moran, the yard superintendent at a highway construction company near Dalton. A sibling was named Oscar, a golden Lab, who joined the family of Jeff Driggins, who is the town electrician at Ashby, nine miles down the road from Dalton.

We've hunted with Stosh since we were pups ourselves, but the first time we got to know Driggins was after someone in our party knocked a wood duck out of the air and it fell among our decoys. All of a sudden, from somewhere else on the lake we lease, this big old white mutt swam up, grabbed our bird, and headed south.

Buddy, not to be outdone, then swam out from our blind, without being ordered, and began bringing in decoys. That's something he got better at with experience. Buddy got bored if his hunters didn't shoot something or couldn't hit anything, so he'd take it on himself to go grab anything that resembled a duck. By the end of the day, our spread of two dozen decoys was generally reduced to about seventeen or eighteen.

But Buddy at his best would go halfway across the lake after a wounded bird. If his hunters dropped six out of one flock, he would methodically bring six back in. And Oscar, who ambushed that woody from us, would gradually join our party, as would Driggins and his sons.

But there was always the added excitement of not knowing exactly what Buddy might do next. Stosh chained him to a boat trailer one day, a big, heavy, steel boat trailer, and then he went away. When he returned, Buddy had dragged that trailer halfway around the campground.

One afternoon, Stosh, J. D., and I were hunting out of Jimmy Peterson's goose pit on a high hill north of Ashby. There was a heavy, steel highway standard pounded deep in the ground next to the pit to warn anyone who might come up to work the field that the pit was there.

We chained Buddy to the pole, and I draped my camouflaged jacket over the sign on the pole. Some mallards flew over, we took a poke at them, and one dropped out of the sky.

That's all it took for old Buddy. He headed out after that bird, and the sign, my jacket, and the whole pole went with him. We later found everything in the next county.

Oscar no longer hunts; first, his hearing went, and now the fields are just too much for the old dog. He prefers to sleep at his home alongside Pelican Lake.

The years took a worse toll on Buddy. He tangled with some barbed wire a few years ago, and his back paw just started to wither away. He was twelve or thirteen years old this fall, twelve or thirteen going on eighty-five, and while the desire was there, he didn't have the stuff anymore. He made one or two retrieves, beautiful but painful to watch at the same time.

He seemed to know it was close to being over. Younger dogs are with us now; my son Chris's Blue and Rudy and Steve Wick's Tubby and Tucker and a new Driggins dog named Buster.

One day this fall, after everyone had gone back to the Cities, Stosh asked Steve to take Buddy to town, to the vet, to be put down. Steve brought Buddy back home, wrapped in an old blanket, and they took him to Jimmy Rylander's place, to a high hill overlooking the famous Lake Christina, where Buddy once watched the canvasbacks by the thousands.

That's where Buddy is now, not far from where Jimmy buried his Shadow. Our old friend is up there on that hill, under a wooden cross that simply says "Buddy."

A Knack for Knowing Things was designed and set in type by Will Powers at the Minnesota Historical Society Press, and printed by Maple Press, York, Pennsylvania.